Language Learning Through Captioned Videos

Mark Feng Teng

NEW YORK AND LONDON

First published 2021
by Routledge
52 Vanderbilt Avenue, New York, NY 10017

and by Routledge
2 Park Square, Milton Park, Abingdon, Oxon, OX14 4RN

Routledge is an imprint of the Taylor & Francis Group, an informa business

© 2021 Taylor & Francis

The right of Mark Feng Teng to be identified as the author of this work has been asserted by him in accordance with sections 77 and 78 of the Copyright, Designs and Patents Act 1988.

All rights reserved. No part of this book may be reprinted or reproduced or utilized in any form or by any electronic, mechanical, or other means, now known or hereafter invented, including photocopying and recording, or in any information storage or retrieval system, without permission in writing from the publishers.

Trademark notice: Product or corporate names may be trademarks or registered trademarks, and are used only for identification and explanation without intent to infringe.

Library of Congress Cataloging-in-Publication Data
A catalog record for this title has been requested

ISBN: 978-0-367-20992-6 (hbk)
ISBN: 978-0-429-26474-0 (ebk)

Typeset in Sabon
by MPS Limited, Dehradun

Contents

Preface		vi
Acknowledgment		viii
1	Introduction to Vocabulary Knowledge and Incidental Vocabulary Acquisition	1
2	Captioned Videos: Multimedia Features, Definitions and Theoretical Frameworks	15
3	Language Learning and Incidental Vocabulary Acquisition From Captioned Videos: Advantages and Disadvantages	35
4	Vocabulary Learning From Captioned Videos for EFL Learners	53
5	Research Methods for Using Captioned Videos in Incidental Vocabulary Acquisition	78
6	Conclusion: Maximizing Vocabulary Learning Performance From Captioned Videos	95
Index		103

Preface

I began learning English in grade one of secondary school. Videos were not available to help me with my English learning at that time. All I had on hand were cassettes. I listened to the cassette tapes repeatedly. Following the economic development in China after the opening-up policy, English became one of the most important languages in China. Consistent with the English fever prevalent at that time, I spent a lot of time learning English. I was finally able to obtain a series of videos after entering university. The video course was called Family Album, the USA, and the videos were captioned. I became obsessed with them as those videos offered a unique perspective for learning English. After watching that series of videos, repeatedly, I became interested in applying the caption technique to improve the learning of English as a foreign language (EFL). Like other EFL contexts, learning English in a Chinese context means that Chinese is the most widely used language and a lack of English input exists. Finding resources, strategies, and techniques to teach and learn English became an important task for me.

I was the type of EFL learner who looked for English videos with captions and watched those videos for an extended period, even several hours a day. I often recommended this technique to my students. I was quite skeptical about the proportion of students who would also do that. But after hearing increased anecdotes from my students over the years about how they have improved their autonomous learning and made huge progress, I became much less skeptical. I increasingly began to promote this technique, for young Chinese learners who were traditionally too dependent on text reading. I found many primary school students did not have very much interest in reading texts; and even when they did, many did not make satisfactory progress in English learning. Demotivation became a common phenomenon in primary school English teaching and learning in China. Through implementing captioned videos in many primary schools and observing how students became more interested in English learning and made progress in vocabulary learning and content comprehension, I became cognizant of the need to maintain and develop strategies for maximizing the benefits of captioned programs or videos.

Like other researchers, I still had one unanswered question about the long-term use of captioned videos. I wondered whether watching captioned programs or videos over longer periods of time would help develop the knowledge and competence required for comprehension of speech while learning the English language without captions. Surely, this technique could not solve all the problems involved in EFL learning. However, considering that many EFL students are "hard of hearing" in the foreign language and learning a foreign language includes both the language and culture, the technique of captioned viewing is needed, through which the richness of language and culture could be made more accessible to EFL students. Captions are not simply a device to enable the deaf and hard-of-hearing to enjoy television programs. Captions were effective at improving EFL students' "hard of hearing" weakness in the foreign language, particularly with vocabulary learning. Within the prevailing internet and multi-media environment, sustaining the effort and motivation needed to gain from captioned viewing becomes easier for learners. Then why not use captioned programs to afford students with more language learning opportunities? This book is a responsive need for language learning from today's multimedia world.

Your best friend,

Mark Feng Teng

Acknowledgment

I thank Professor Robert Vanderplank for his helpful and valuable comments on reading the manuscript for this book. I also thank Professor Robert Vanderplank for his permission on using his developed models in his book on captioned videos (2016). The author acknowledges the following sources of materials and is grateful for the permissions granted. Extracts from Teng (2020) and (2019) by permission of Routledge and Springer.

1 Introduction to Vocabulary Knowledge and Incidental Vocabulary Acquisition

Teachers of English as a foreign language (EFL) recognize the importance of vocabulary in learning a language. Vocabulary is the foundation for learning a language. Without a sufficient vocabulary, claiming fluency in a foreign language is impossible. Schmitt (2010) proposed that little information can be conveyed without grammar, and nothing can be expressed without words. This assertion reflects my personal experience with EFL learning; I learned several useful keywords and expressions and managed to communicate with native speakers. Vocabulary knowledge became the foundation of my grammar and syntax learning.

The importance of learning vocabulary is commonly acknowledged among teachers. Building a rich repertoire of vocabulary knowledge is necessary, particularly for EFL students who wish to develop fluency and expression in English. Nearly everyone—from beginning learners in English to professors in academia—has experienced the frustration of not having the right word immediately available within one's lexicon. Occasionally these occurrences are a matter of not being able to recall the right word; sometimes we just do not *know* the right word. While reading a newspaper or homework assignment, running across words whose meanings elude us can be frustrating. Building a vocabulary level essential to one's reading and communication needs should be a personal goal for each learner.

Students instinctively recognize the importance of learning vocabulary, as evidenced by their often carrying dictionaries but not grammar books. Students also generally understand that a small vocabulary can inhibit effective communication. A larger vocabulary leads to better performance in listening, speaking, reading, and writing. While first-language (L1) learners acquire words incidentally through reading (Nagy, Anderson, & Herman, 1987), whether incidental vocabulary learning is effective for second-language (L2) learners remains a vexing

2 Introduction to Vocabulary Knowledge

question. Can incidental L2 vocabulary learning be as effective as explicit word learning? If so, how? If not, how can incidental vocabulary acquisition be maximized? Exploring these issues should be interesting, but first we need to define what a word is.

What is a Word?

A word includes three aspects: form, meaning, and use. According to Nation (2013), a word's form involves its pronunciation (spoken form), spelling (written form), and any smaller parts that make up that particular word (such as a prefix, root, and suffix). An example of word parts can be exemplified by the word *uncommunicative*, in which the prefix un- means "negative" or "opposite," communicate is the root word, and -ive is a suffix denoting that someone or something is able to do something. The different components go together to refer to someone or something who/that cannot communicate and is hence *uncommunicative*. Nation (2013) stated that meaning encompasses how form and meaning work together—in other words, the concept, the items to which it refers, and the associations that come to mind when people think about a specific word or expression. Use, as Nation (2013) noted, involves the grammatical functions of a word or phrase, the collocations that normally accompany it, and any constraints on its use in terms of frequency, level, and so forth. Nation (2013) further declared that form, meaning, and use each separately contains three components, and each component includes a receptive and productive dimension. As such, learning these three aspects for each word or phrase actually involves 18 types of lexical knowledge, as summarized in Table 1.1.

Learners exhibit individual differences in acquiring vocabulary knowledge. Some learners excel in the grammatical functions of particular words or phrases, while others may have a greater knowledge of English word parts. Teachers' vocabulary instruction should be built on an understanding of learners' strengths and weaknesses. For example, many students may be adept at recognizing meaning in terms of concepts and referents. However, if learners have not seen particular words or phrases before, then they may be less able to recognize them when the words are spoken or less prepared to pronounce them when read aloud. Sometimes students are weak at recognizing particular types of vocabulary usage. For example, young learners might use a particular word or expression that may be colloquial and rarely appropriate in formal contexts, such as in a speech.

Yet if teachers are aware of students' strengths and weaknesses in English vocabulary, then they have a starting place when attempting

Table 1.1 What is Involved in Knowing a Word?

Aspect	Component	Receptive Knowledge	Productive Knowledge
Form	Spoken	What does the word sound like?	How is the word pronounced?
	Written	What does the word look like?	How is the word written and spelled?
	Word parts	What parts in this word are recognizable?	What word parts are needed to express the meaning?
Meaning	Form and meaning	What meaning does this word form signal?	What word form can be used to express this meaning?
	Concepts and references	What is included in this concept?	What items can the concept refer to?
	Associations	What other words does this word make people think of?	What other words could people use instead of this one?
Use	Grammatical functions	In what patterns does the word occur?	In what patterns must people use this word?
	Collocations	Which words or types of words occur along with this one?	Which words or types of words must people use with this one?
	Constraints (Register, frequency...)	Where, when, and how often would people expect to encounter this word?	Where, when, and how often can people use this word?

Source: Adapted from Nation (2013).

to expand students' knowledge. When reviewing the information in Table 1.1, teachers may find it challenging to approach the task of teaching English vocabulary. If so, they are not alone; there is much for teachers and students to learn to understand and use words and phrases correctly in different situations. This chapter does not claim to cover every aspect but instead aims to help teachers understand important issues from recent vocabulary research and theory so they may approach incidental vocabulary teaching and learning in a principled, thoughtful way.

How can Our Learners Expand Vocabulary Knowledge?

Learning English vocabulary is a cumulative process. Lexical items are continually being added to existing vocabulary lists. In a book by Lessard-Clouston (2013), he pointed out that this circumstance is most evident with computer-related vocabularies, partially because of the development of the internet, e-mail, and web browsers. Helping learners expand their vocabulary knowledge is important and can be accomplished in many ways. As a non-native English speaker, I have been learning vocabulary for many years, but I am still a learner because English vocabulary continually evolves. Occasionally, I come across an unknown word or phrase (or a new usage for one I already know) in print, online, or via radio or television. I then stop to consider what the term might mean in that particular context and make a guess. If I have a dictionary close by, I will check it for that word or phrase; if I am at my computer, I will consult an online dictionary. When watching English-language videos or programs without captions, I am always afraid that I will miss some information. Even though missing that information does not prevent me from comprehending the content, I nevertheless want to learn every word. But when I stop watching the video, I miss more information. However, with the help of captions, I can understand more aural information. I also continue to ponder how to learn and use words. To a certain extent, this technique expands my vocabulary knowledge.

English vocabulary requires form, meaning, and use but also involves layers of meaning connected to the roots of words (Nation & Meara, 2010). Teaching vocabulary does not simply call for the explicit teaching of individual words; it also involves the use of lexical knowledge. The most important goal is to expand learners' vocabulary knowledge. One of the reasons students often fail to reach their vocabulary-related goals is a lack of assistance in understanding spoken and written discourse. Perhaps some students do not recognize the importance of out-of-classroom vocabulary learning. Some also need to become autonomous vocabulary learners by referencing various resources or types of language input.

One would be remiss to discuss vocabulary knowledge without considering the degree to which individuals differ in their ability (and interest) to learn words. The number of words learned vary greatly among students, as documented in previous studies (e.g., Webb & Chang, 2012). Some students may work harder than others. Additional influencing factors include one's aptitude and initial language proficiency. For example, as documented in one of my studies (Teng, 2019a), some students with a larger vocabulary or better English proficiency may make relatively large gains during captioned video viewing. Hence, monitoring vocabulary size and helping students improve their lexical development is extremely important.

Can students expand their vocabulary knowledge? In short, yes. As an EFL learner, I understand that progress is the most powerful stimulus for learning. Students can only learn a small proportion of frequent word families through explicit classroom instruction; they must learn more words independently outside class. The greater the amount of input, the more often students will encounter unknown or partially known words. Repeated encounters will help students develop word-related knowledge and strengthen their confidence in learning vocabulary. For instance, as documented in some of my studies, reading while listening to graded reader audiobooks can increase EFL learners' potential to develop lexical knowledge (Teng, 2018b). Marginal glosses can help EFL learners better understand new words while reading (Teng, 2019c). Watching L2 TV programs or videos, particularly captioned videos, may further expand learners' potential to increase their vocabulary knowledge (Teng, 2019d).

What is Incidental Vocabulary Acquisition?

Incidental vocabulary acquisition refers to the learning of words or expressions through reading or listening activities without a conscious intention to commit target items to memory (Hulstijn, 2013). For instance, learners can pick up unknown words while engaging in communicative activities with partners. You will probably have no difficulty recalling something that happened to you a couple of days ago, but it may be hard to recall the details of an incident from a few years ago. These examples briefly illustrate the challenges associated with incidentally recalling factual knowledge, including words, dates, events, and explanations.

In contrast to incidental vocabulary learning, intentional vocabulary learning refers to learners' deliberate attempts to commit words to memory using rehearsal techniques, such as rote learning or when preparing for a school test (Hulstijn, 2013). One example of the difference between intentional and incidental learning is that intentional learners were told in advance that they would be tested afterwards on materials to which they had been exposed. Learners in the incidental learning condition were not told they would be tested later. In this case, incidental and intentional learning respectively pertain to

6 *Introduction to Vocabulary Knowledge*

whether learners were notified they would be completing a post-test after the intervention, as this advance notice may have compelled the learners to deliberately attempt to commit target words to memory.

Research Issues in Incidental Vocabulary Acquisition

To better understand incidental vocabulary acquisition, this section delineates critical issues involved in vocabulary research. These components can contextualize the various factors shaping incidental vocabulary acquisition.

Vocabulary Knowledge is a Rich and Complex Construct

Learners need a large vocabulary along with knowledge of each individual lexical item to functionally use a language well. In one of my studies (Teng, 2018a), one's quality or depth of vocabulary knowledge is as important as vocabulary size. Many teachers and learners might consider a lexical item "learned" if the spoken/written form and meaning are known. The form-meaning link is the most essential lexical feature. We also need to understand how lexical items can be used productively. Depth of knowledge can be conceptualized in several ways. One is overall proficiency with a word, ranging from absolutely no knowledge to complete mastery. This developmental conceptualization is typically measured along a scale, such as via the Vocabulary Knowledge Scale (Paribakht & Wesche, 1997) and a 4-stage scale used by Schmitt and Zimmerman (2002).

A second means of conceptualizing vocabulary knowledge involves deconstructing it into discrete elements, otherwise known as the "component" or "dimension" approach. For example, Nation (2013) specified the kinds of knowledge one must possess about a word to use it well. The original list included eight types of word knowledge: spoken form, written form, grammatical patterns, collocations, frequency, appropriateness (register), meaning, and associations.

Vocabulary Learning is Inherently Incremental

Incidental vocabulary acquisition is incremental, both in terms of acquiring adequate vocabulary and individual lexical items. The gradual acquisition of increasingly larger lexicons was well illustrated in a study by Henriksen (2008), who measured the L2 vocabulary size of Danish EFL students. She found consistent improvement in

Introduction to Vocabulary Knowledge 7

vocabulary size across increasing grades among L1 and L2 students, despite such growth being achieved over an extended period. Unsurprisingly, she also discovered that L1 scores were larger than L2 scores, even though the L1 test included many low-frequency items compared to the L2 test.

One component of word knowledge that has been studied extensively is meaning (Schmitt, 2010). Teng (2018a) suggested that receptive mastery generally develops before productive mastery, although this may not be the case for every item. This pattern has been illustrated in studies comparing the number of words known productively versus receptively. For example, Laufer (2005) compared learners' productive test scores on L1–L2 recall tests as a percentage of their receptive test scores on L2–L1 translation tests. She found productive/receptive ratios ranging from 16% at the 5,000-frequency level to 35% at the 2,000-frequency level, while Fan (2000) found a range from 53% to 81% (mean: 69.2%) for words taken from the 2,000, 3,000, and University Word List levels.

In previous books (Schmitt, 2010; Webb & Nation, 2017), vocabulary acquisition has been described as incremental in numerous ways. First, lexical knowledge consists of different types of vocabulary knowledge. Multiple aspects of vocabulary knowledge may not be mastered simultaneously. Second, each vocabulary knowledge aspect may develop along an incline. Word learning is incremental, as is the acquisition of individual word knowledge aspects. Third, each form of vocabulary knowledge varies in the associated degree of receptive/productive mastery. Taken together, findings indicate that vocabulary learning is a complicated and gradual process. The initial form–meaning link cannot guarantee subsequent development of vocabulary knowledge. If only a single vocabulary knowledge aspect such as meaning can be measured, then results must be interpreted through an incremental learning perspective.

Vocabulary Form is Important

Learning a lexical item is conceptualized as learning its form and meaning (Schmitt, 2010). Learning meaning is an essential initial step in vocabulary acquisition; however, learning vocabulary also involves developing a link between form and meaning. This form–meaning linkage is the minimum requirement for knowing a word. If a learner knows a word's lexical form but not its meaning, then they will not be able to communicate using the term. Likewise, if a learner knows a word's meaning but not its corresponding form, then they will not be able to apply the term in a text. EFL vocabulary teaching materials attempt to focus on this form-meaning link, and most tests measure it in one way or another. However, in some cases, meaning is stressed as the key component of this link while downplaying the form element. In fact, it can be difficult for EFL learners to memorize word forms. Laufer (1998) studied words with similar forms and noted that learners found certain similarities confusing, especially words that were similar apart from their suffixes (e.g., *comprehensive/comprehensible*) and for vowels (e.g., *adopt/adapt*). Learners may also find L2 words that have a similar form to be perplexing; Schmitt (2008) labeled this phenomenon *orthographic neighborhoods*. For example, learners may find the word *poll* easy to learn, but similar forms in English (e.g., *pool, polo, pollen, pole, pall, pill*) may confuse them.

Hence, form is pivotal in that it is the basic step leading to meaning acquisition. Form is mainly acquired through exposure. Vocabulary researchers or classroom practitioners should not take the orthographic/phonological mastery of word form for granted; rather, they should consider it an essential (and sometimes problematic) component of lexical learning. In addition, they must carefully consider form–meaning aspects of the target vocabulary when designing vocabulary-focused studies.

Vocabulary Attrition and Long-term Retention

As described by Schmitt (2010), vocabulary acquisition is not a simple linear affair, with only incremental advancement and no backsliding. It is normal for learners to forget the words they have learned. Forgetting (also called attrition) is a natural part of learning. The acquisition of vocabulary knowledge is continually in flux, with both learning and forgetting occurring until a word has been mastered and "fixed" in one's memory (Reynolds, 2020). Attrition can also occur even if learners are familiar with certain vocabulary. When one does not use a second language for a long time or stops a course of language study, attrition is normal. Yet controversy exists around attrition, largely due to difficulties in measuring vocabulary retention. Lexical knowledge, particularly for low-frequency words, seems more susceptible to attrition than other linguistic aspects, such as phonology or grammar.

Attrition is a logical consequence of a lack of practice because vocabulary is learned through individual units. Further, no series of rules is available for vocabulary learning. Attrition in terms of receptive knowledge may not be drastic, whereas productive mastery is more likely to be lost. The rate of attrition is connected to a language learner's working memory capacity and proficiency level. Learners with greater working memory capacity and language proficiency may be likely to retain more residual vocabulary knowledge. In a book, Schmitt (2010) described how attrition manifests in different learners. For example, most attrition occurred within the first two years of language learning and then levelled off. One of my studies (Teng, 2018b) revealed that once vocabulary is learned, it does not seem to disappear completely. Therefore, we may need to view attrition relative to lexical access as normal, although lexical knowledge may not vanish entirely.

Engagement in Vocabulary Acquisition

A common idea is that the more a learner engages with a new word, the more likely they are to learn it. Several studies have attempted to define this notion of engagement more precisely. For example, the depth/levels of processing hypothesis laid the important groundwork: presumably, the more attention given to an item, and the more manipulation involved with that item, the greater the chances the item will be remembered (Craik & Lockhart, 1972). Laufer and Hulstijn (2001) refined this notion, suggesting that vocabulary learning consists of three components: need, search, and evaluation. Need includes the internal or external requirements of completing some tasks, such as knowing a particular word and understanding a passage. Search represents one's attempt to locate necessary information (e.g., looking up the meaning of a certain word in a dictionary). Evaluation refers to comparing a word, or information about a word, to the context of use to determine the word's suitability. Evidence has shown that learners drafting compositions remembered a set of target words better than those who saw the words in a reading comprehension task, and learners who supplied missing target words in gaps in the text remembered more of those words than learners who read marginal glosses. Students in the "better learning" case were more involved in their learning, according to Laufer and Hulstijn's (2001) scheme. Therefore, tasks containing relatively more need, search, and evaluation elements were more effective.

Overall, we may need to consider which vocabulary learning activities may lead to greater exposure, attention, manipulation, and engagement. Schmitt (2008) put forth the term "engagement" to encompass all potential aspects of learner involvement. Vocabulary can be acquired when learners engage in incidental learning-oriented tasks. Vocabulary learning should also entail active engagement in learning tasks and computer technology. Vocabulary learning is part of a cyclical process in which a higher level of self-regulated learning leads to greater engagement with and use of vocabulary learning strategies, which in turn yield better mastery of word form, meaning, and use. Enhanced vocabulary learning can then be self-appraised and later oriented to better fine-tune self-regulated vocabulary learning (Teng & Reynolds, 2019). Any technique that can help learners become more engaged with vocabulary learning is therefore fundamental for teachers and learners.

What should L2/EFL Teachers Do?

Teachers can consider many facets to encourage students' meaningful progress in lexical development. For example, we need a principled approach to teaching vocabulary. The direct teaching of vocabulary in the classroom likely accounts for only a small portion of vocabulary learning outcomes. In terms of teachers' roles, Webb and Nation (2017) proposed nine key aspects to support learners' lexical development: (1) select the words to be learned; (2) raise awareness of the vocabulary learning program; (3) teach words deliberately; (4) choose materials containing target vocabulary; (5) design activities to create opportunities for vocabulary use; (6) include fluency development activities; (7) measure progress; (8) train students in learning strategies; and (9) evaluate and modify strategies.

Teachers should also build an awareness of the language problems learners face due to a lack of vocabulary knowledge. Many learners encounter obstacles ranging from not understanding a reading passage to being unable to express themselves accurately when writing or speaking because of too many unknown vocabulary words/items. Therefore, teachers need to consider not only the vocabulary in the *material* but also the vocabulary *needed for the task.*

It takes time to choose key vocabulary items to be taught. Designing appropriate written exercises to encourage students to retrieve newly learned vocabulary lesson after lesson requires extensive time, too. Frequency is an important factor in incidental vocabulary learning. Peters (2014) reported that "An increase in frequency resulted in higher recall scores of the target item to be learned" (p. 89). However, previous studies did not pinpoint the exact number of times a learner needed to encounter a word to establish a form-meaning link. In light of this, Chen and Truscott (2010) argued, "The goal of research should not be to identify a definitive number of exposures needed, but rather to understand a complex process involving multiple, interacting variables" (p. 694). EFL/L2 learners need more exposure to acquiring word knowledge; thus, teachers should be mindful of the frequency of difficult words when preparing materials.

In addition, simply inferring the meaning of unknown words is challenging for EFL/L2 learners. Teachers should supplement the elaboration of word processing for incidental vocabulary acquisition by designing vocabulary activities. For example, teachers can provide the meanings of target words along with relevant exercises in which learners must process these words. The use of captioned vidoes is also an effective means (Teng, 2019e). Providing elaborate word processing can help learners establish a more refined and durable form–meaning relationship (Eckerth & Tavakoli, 2012; Laufer & Rozovski-Roitblat, 2011). Learners should also engage in the rehearsal of newly learned words (Teng, 2019b). Teachers can help students review target words. Acquired word knowledge has been shown to suffer a substantial decay in gains over a one-month period (Waring & Takaki, 2003). To curb precipitous declines in word retention, teachers can provide opportunities for learners to recycle target words frequently.

Vocabulary Learning through Audiovisual Input: A Trend in Incidental Vocabulary Acquisition

This chapter introduces the concept of a word, as well as the importance of incidental vocabulary acquisition. This chapter also introduces five research issues for incidental vocabulary acquisition. Relevant suggestions for teachers are also provided. Vocabulary researchers need to be aware of the various lexical characteristics and be able to make conscious and principled decisions about which characteristics to control for in their studies. Careful consideration at the initial stages of research design may be the best insurance against a study later becoming contaminated by unwanted lexical behavior which confounds interpretation of the results.

Research gives us little insight into the precise mechanisms by which incidental vocabulary acquisition takes place. Although we describe unconscious picking up of the vocabulary from reading or other activities as incidental learning, the creation of such occasions in schools or homes represents intention on the part of educators and parents. Incidental vocabulary acquisition is a slow and error-prone process with partial vocabulary gains (Teng, 2018b, 2019b; Brown, Waring & Donkaewbua, 2008). Readers do not always notice unfamiliar words when reading a text. If they do, guessing the meaning is not always possible. Moreover, many EFL/L2 learners possess poor inferencing skills. Thus, in terms of incidental vocabulary acquisition, learners may process new vocabulary only superficially or even skip new words altogether and produce little knowledge of new words.

Hence, as Teng (2019de) asserted, teachers or researchers could contemplate using captioned videos which can compel learners to process new vocabulary elaborately. In literature on incidental vocabulary learning, the use of audiovisual input for learning vocabulary is highlighted (see Chapter 4). Lexical growth can be achieved through large amounts of spoken input. Although spoken input contains fewer encounters with lower frequency words than written input, it is appropriate for EFL learners with limited language proficiency level. Based on Rodgers and Webb (2011), if L2 television is watched regularly, the number of unknown words that are encountered will increase and the potential for learning will rise sharply. Hence, while audiovisual input might not provide as high of a proportion of lower-frequency words as written input, the greater amount of time spent in exposure to audiovisual input might actually lead to a similar number of encounters with low-frequency words. Vocabulary learning through audiovisual input becomes a trend in incidental vocabulary acquisition. For example, bi-modal input contained in the captioned videos can encourage the learners to read the online text, look up the meaning of any words from the verbal and non-verbal input, comprehend the content, and finally, learn the new words. The next chapter will focus on explaining the definition and frameworks for captioned videos.

References

Brown, R., Waring, R., & Donkaewbua, S. (2008). Incidental vocabulary acquisition from reading, reading-while-listening, and listening to stories. *Reading in a Foreign Language*, 20(2), 136–163.

Chen, C., & Truscott, J. (2010). The effects of repetition and L1 lexicalization on incidental vocabulary acquisition. *Applied Linguistics*, 31(1), 693–713.

Lessard-Clouston, M. (2013). *Teaching vocabulary*. Alexandria, VA: TESOL International Association.

Craik, F. I. M., & Lockhart, R. S. (1972). Levels of processing: A framework for memory research. *Journal of Verbal Learning and Verbal Behavior*, 11(1), 671–684.

Eckerth, J., & Tavakoli, P. (2012). The effects of word frequency and elaboration of word processing on incidental L2 vocabulary acquisition through reading. *Language Teaching Research*, 16(2), 227–252.

Fan, M. (2000). How big is the gap and how to narrow it? An investigation into the active and passive vocabulary knowledge of L2 learners. *RELC Journal* 31(2), 105–119.

Henriksen, B. (2008). Declarative lexical knowledge. In Albrechtsen, D., Haastrup, K., & Henriksen, B. (Eds.), *Vocabulary and writing in a first and second language* (pp. 22–66). Basingstoke: Palgrave Macmillan.

Hulstijn, J. H. (2013). Incidental learning in second language acquisition. In C. A. Chapelle (Ed.), *The encyclopedia of applied linguistics* (pp. 2632–2640). Chichester: Wiley-Blackwell.

Laufer, B. (1998). The development of passive and active vocabulary in a second language: Same or different? *Applied Linguistics*, 12(1), 255–271.

Laufer, B. (2005). Focus on form in second language vocabulary learning. *EUROSLA Yearbook*, 5(1), 223–250.

Laufer, B., & Hulstijn, J. (2001). Incidental vocabulary acquisition in a second language: The construct of task-induced involvement. *Applied Linguistics*, 22, 1–26.

Laufer, B., & Rozovski-Roitblat, B. (2011). Incidental vocabulary acquisition: The effects of task type, word occurrence and their combination. *Language Teaching Research*, 15(4), 391–411.

Nagy, W. E., Anderson, R. C., & Herman, P. A. (1987). Learning word meanings from context during normal reading. *American Educational Research Journal*, 24(2), 237–270.

Nation, I. S. P. (2013). *Learning vocabulary in another language* (2nd ed.). Cambridge: Cambridge University Press.

Nation, I. S. P., & Meara, P. (2010). Vocabulary. In N. Schmitt (Ed.), *An introduction to applied linguistics* (2nd ed., pp. 252–267). London, England: Hodder Education.

Paribakht, T. S., & Wesche, M. (1997). Vocabulary enhancement activities and reading for meaning in second language vocabulary acquisition. In Coady, J. & Huckin, T. (Eds.), *Second language vocabulary acquisition* (pp. 174–200). Cambridge: Cambridge University Press.

Peters, E. (2014). The effects of repetition and time of post-test administration on EFL learners' form recall of single words and collocations. *Language Teaching Research*, 18(1), 75–94.

Reynolds, B. L. (2020). The effects of nonce words, frequency, contextual richness, and L2 vocabulary knowledge on the incidental acquisition of vocabulary through reading: More than a replication of Zahar et al. (2001) & Tekmen and Daloğlu (2006). *IRAL-International Review of Applied Linguistics in Language Teaching*, 58(1), 75–102. DOI: https://doi.org/10.1515/iral-2015-0115.

Rodgers, M. P. H., & Webb, S. (2011). Narrowing viewing: the vocabulary in related television programs. *TESOL Quarterly*, 45(4), 689–717.

Schmitt, N. (2008). Review article: Instructed second language vocabulary learning. *Language Teaching Research*, 12(3), 329–363.

Schmitt, N. (2010). *Researching vocabulary: A vocabulary research manual*. Basingstoke, England: Palgrave Macmillan.

Schmitt, N., & Zimmerman, C. B. (2002). Derivative word forms: What do learners know? *TESOL Quarterly*, 36(2), 145–171.

Teng, F. (2018a). A learner-based approach of applying online reading to improve learner autonomy and lexical knowledge. *Spanish Journal of Applied Linguistics*, *31*, 104–134.

Teng, F. (2018b). Incidental vocabulary acquisition from reading-only and reading-while-listening: A multi-dimensional approach. *Innovation in Language Learning and Teaching*, *12*(3), 274–288.

Teng, F. (2019a). Incidental vocabulary learning for primary school students: The effects of L2 caption type and word exposure frequency. *The Australian Educational Researcher*, *46*(1), 113–136.

Teng, F. (2019b). The effects of context and word exposure frequency on incidental vocabulary acquisition and retention through reading. *The Language Learning Journal*, *47*(2), 145–158.

Teng, F. (2019c). Retention of new words learned incidentally from reading: Word exposure frequency, L1 marginal glosses, and their combination. *Language Teaching Research*. https://journals.sagepub.com/doi/10.1177/1362168819829026.

Teng, F. (2019d). *Maximizing the potential of captions for primary school ESL students' comprehension of English-language videos*. Computer Assisted Language Learning, *32*(7), 665–691. Doi: 10.1080/09588221.2018.1532912.

Teng, F. (2019e). *The effects of video caption types and advance organizers on incidental L2 collocation learning*. Computers & Education, *142*, 103655. Doi:10.1016/j.compedu.2019.103655.

Teng, F., & Reynolds, B. L. (2019). Effects of individual and group metacognitive prompts on EFL reading comprehension and incidental vocabulary learning. *PLOS One*. https://journals.plos.org/plosone/article?id=10.1371/journal.pone.0215902.

Waring, R., & Takaki, M. (2003). At what rate do learners learn and retain new vocabulary from reading a graded reader? *Reading in a Foreign Language*, *15*(2), 130–163.

Webb, S., & Chang, A. C.-S. (2012). Second language vocabulary growth. *RELC Journal*, *43*(1), 113–126.

Webb, S., & Nation, P. (2017). *How vocabulary is learned*. Oxford: Oxford University Press.

2 Captioned Videos
Multimedia Features, Definitions and Theoretical Frameworks

Discerning practical and effective ways to enhance EFL students' vocabulary is essential in foreign language education. Vocabulary is the primary building block for learning a foreign language (Teng, 2019a; Webb & Nation, 2017). However, teaching students English as a foreign (EFL) or second language (L2) is not an easy task. Learners may lack the attentional control to assimilate the given term for subsequent use (Koolstra & Beentjes, 1999). Learners may also find it difficult to establish a form-meaning link, defined as "the assignment of meaning to the orthographical representation of the word" (Rott, 2007, p. 166). Earlier research has revealed that incidental vocabulary acquisition—namely, the learning of a new word or expression without conscious intent to commit the element to memory, e.g., "picking up" an unknown word from language input (Hulstijn, 2013)—was challenging for students learning English as a foreign language (EFL) (Reynolds & Teng, 2020; Teng, 2018, 2019b; Teng & Reynolds, 2019; Webb & Chang, 2015). Limited language processing during exposure to language input may not allow learners to derive a term's meaning and construct a form-meaning link (Hulstijn, 2001).

Captioned videos may offer a new perspective in exploring incidental vocabulary acquisition (Montero Perez, Peters, & Desmet, 2018). Educators worldwide have generally acknowledged the potential for using captioned videos to enhance EFL/L2 learners' vocabulary development, an important part of English language learning that carries long-term implications for future academic development. Captions, which turn videos into a storybook with a stream of written text presented synchronously with video and audio reinforcement, were originally developed for the deaf or hard-of-hearing (Danan, 2004). Scholars contended that the cognitive process involved in watching captioned videos was not as overwhelming as the process for bi-modal input. Captioning served as a support, offering multiple representations of the same information to learners (Vanderplank, 2016a). Research also found that learners used captioned videos to "increase their attention, improve processing, reinforce prior knowledge, and analyze language" (Winke, Gass, & Sydorenko, 2010, p. 65). In a meta-analysis study (Montero Perez, Van Den Noortgate, & Desmet, 2013), captioned videos were found to have a large effect on learners' listening comprehension and vocabulary learning.

Captioned videos are informative because they supply the learners with different channels of information, including the pictorial information, the original sound track, and the on-screen text in the same language as the sound track (Teng, 2019c). Captioned videos are thus becoming increasingly common as a tool for teaching and learning English, likely because of the expanding accessibility to authentic videos via DVD, YouTube, ViewPoint, and mobile phone apps. Audio-visual materials enhanced with captions represent a powerful pedagogical tool believed to improve vocabulary learning (Montero Perez et al., 2018). Although videos may also provide rich materials to learners, learners may not perceive the language and images in the video as opportunities for language uptake (Danan, 2004). Based on multimedia principle—i.e., "people learn better from words and pictures than from words alone" (Fletcher & Tobias, 2005, p. 117)—captioned videos are expected to result in learners' greater depth of language processing and better recall of new words (Peters, Heynen, & Puimege, 2016). In addition, videos can be easily captioned by classroom practitioners and curriculum developers using software such as Adobe Premier, MAGpie, or iMovie. Many schools across the world, eager to enhance students' English performance, are beginning to offer hybrid or blended-instruction courses in which some instruction is conducted within the classroom and some occurs independently outside the classroom (Teng, 2017). Such classes naturally incorporate more online content, which often includes captioned videos. Evidence in two eye-tracking studies (Montero Perez et al., 2015; Winke, Gass, & Sydorenko, 2013) supports that learners increased their attention to words while watching the captioned videos. However, studies in using captioned videos for incidental vocabulary acquisition have yielded varying results (Jelani & Boers, 2018; Montero Perez, Peters, Clarebout, & Desmet, 2014; Sydorenko, 2010). One explanation is due to the different test types in measuring a series of different components, ranging from word form recognition to proper use in context. Other studies have challenged the use of captioned videos by showing that students were too reliant on reading captions and most ignored the soundtrack (Latifi, Mobalegh, & Mohammadi, 2011). Similarly, Diao,

Chandler, and Sweller (2007) found that while watching captioned videos, L2 learners depended too much on reading on-screen text; they became passive to incoming information, which led to superficial learning. Taylor (2005) argued that simultaneous presentation of pictures (animations) and words (on-screen text or captions) may overwhelm L2 learners if they have a low language proficiency to process audiovisual material. Other factors, including differences in vocabulary knowledge (Winke, Gass, & Sydorenko, 2013), learners' English profiencicy (Teng, 2019c), age (Muñoz, 2017), affect language learning through captioned videos.

According to multimedia learning principle (Mayer, 2001), effective learning can take place when multimedia learning helps learners decrease extraneous cognitive load during learning and orient learner's attention toward germane materials, thereby increasing germane (schema related) cognitive load. Based on this theoretical conceptualization, the combination of verbal and non-verbal input in the captioned videos may prompt learners to perceive, comprehend, subsume, and merge new information into their mental system (Plass & Jones, 2005). Ineffective learning occurs when learners' attention is distracted. For example, learning vocabulary from English videos alone may not help learners build a link for retrieval of meanings. Learners may need some visual aids to construct stronger meaning representations for retrieval. For example, there is a need to provide non-verbal aids to enhance vocabulary learning. Hence, L2 captions, a type of on-screen textual information in learners' target language, can lead to better processing and recall because of the triple association between image, sound, and text (Danan, 2004). Given international research interest in captioned videos, this chapter explores issues in EFL incidental vocabulary acquisition through watching captioned videos. Specifically, this chapter provides insight into (1) the types of captioning on incidental vocabulary acquisition, (2) definitions of captioned videos, (3) frameworks or models related to the adoption of captioned videos. This chapter aims to help researchers and classroom practitioners understand the essence of research scholarship on using captioned videos for EFL learners' incidental vocabulary acquisition.

Definiton of Captions

We usually regard television as a medium for entertainment and information. The amount of mental effort devoted to learning from TV programs has been deemed a key factor influencing individuals' learning outcomes. Learners' effort or investment in processing materials depends on their mental schema. For instance, complex, ambiguous, or new material that does not easily match one's existing mental schema requires greater effort to process. By contrast, learners may devote little mental effort to easier material. Television is a minimally demanding medium compared to reading print; however, learners may still consider television a limited resource for language learning. Rodgers (2013) studied incidental vocabulary learning and explored learners' attitudes toward captioned videos in a Japanese multimedia learning context. He suggested that TV programs may not be suitable for language learning because some programs contain massive quantities of input to be processed. The potential benefits of audiovisual materials for language learning may be negated by the nature of television as a complex, dynamic, and fast-paced resource. Teachers and learners thus need captions to help process TV language input effectively.

So, what are captions and how did they come about? The technical background would require a lengthy history; therefore, only key issues are summarized here. Initially, the primary purpose of captions was to accommodate the needs of the deaf and hard of hearing. Yet researchers have since highlighted captions as an important technique for foreign language learners without hearing disabilities. Over the years, several terms have been used to refer to captions. The standard term in North America is "closed captions," as captions are not automatically visible but can be revealed through the closed-caption decoder built into one's television. Some have referred to captions as "subtitles," although the two terms are distinct. For our purposes in an ESL context, "captions" refer to the on-screen text in students' native language combined with a second-language soundtrack in the video; "subtitles" refer to the on-screen text in a learner's original language combined with a soundtrack in the same language. In this book, I describe the differences in these terms but use "captions" for the sake of simplicity.

We are fortunate that captions are available for learning a foreign language. Many learners find themselves "hard-of-listening" when learning a target language (Vanderplank, 1988, p. 272). Captioning is an effective means of making films and TV programs more accessible to language learners. One benefit of captioned videos is that the combination of visual, contextual, and nonverbal input provides foreign language learners with simultaneous visual and aural stimuli. Such a technique inhibits the lack of comprehension resulting from merely spoken input. Captions visualize auditory information in the foreign language learners hear in the video. This additional cognitive processing explains why captions promote language comprehension. Vanderplank (2016a) presented four axioms guiding captioned television in language learning:

- Captions transform general televised output, such as documentaries and sitcoms, into rich language resources for learners.
- Captions help balance visual and verbal elements in a TV program.
- Captions have a liberating effect on teachers and learners in terms of choice, control, and responsibility.
- Captions enable learners to watch programs in a native-speaker manner.

Captions are becoming more popular in language learning. However, some problems persist for learners and teachers. The first issue concerns learners' attention or engagement. As described in Chapter 1, engagement is an important factor in vocabulary learning. Captions can help learners become more involved in watching a foreign-language program. Engagement (i.e., the effort learners invest in processing the language presented in captions) has a major influence on the learning outcomes derived from captioned videos. The second issue concerns the nature of the medium. Learners may become more focused on the leisure activity (i.e., "watching TV") rather than the content; that is, some learners may view these videos as pure forms of entertainment rather than education. As mentioned above, learners generally perceive TV programs as easy to understand while printed materials seem difficult. It is therefore necessary to carefully design programs to ensure clear educational messaging. Language editing for captions is also important. Only learners who put forth sufficient effort to comprehend captions will derive optimal educational benefit. The third issue concerns a lack of awareness about using TV programs as a resource for language learning and teaching. This knowledge gap may be due to the nature of television as a dynamic and verbal medium. Multiple factors, including institutional policies and teachers' attitudes, may further discourage the use of TV programs in teaching and learning. Hence, we should be more diligent about raising awareness of the value of using captions in this setting. Teachers should attend to caption quality, select materials based on students' proficiency, and consider the balance between reading and listening requirements.

Frameworks Supporting Captioned Viewing for Language Learning

This section outlines several frameworks that support captioned viewing for language learning. These frameworks relate to various dimensions, including second-language acquisition, cognitive load, and working memory.

The Input Hypothesis

The input hypothesis, developed by Krashen (1989), has played an integral role in second-language acquisition theory. According to this hypothesis, students learn language by understanding input slightly above their current level of competence. For example, L2 learners acquire language through meaningful conversation slightly above their present understanding, coined "i + 1." Such learning is context-based and not learned through formal instruction of reading or grammar. In this regard, L2 learning differs from L1 learning because authentic communicative situations in a second language are more challenging. Compared to language learning that is conscious, deliberate, or more formal, L2 acquisition is subconscious, incidental, and natural.

In L2 learning, the notion of consciousness has received extensive attention. Per Schmidt (1990), consciousness is essential to language learning outcomes. In relation to the subconscious perspective of the input hypothesis, two common viewpoints are that language is learned through either (a) explicit instruction and deliberate drills and practice with a linguistic structure or (b) output practice that can be facilitated by peer feedback (Swain & Lapkin, 2001). Language learning from captioned videos is akin to Krashen's (1989) language acquisition model because such learning is contextualized in social and communicative contexts. Watching TV programs requires a low affective filter and positive attitudinal and motivational factors because these programs provide viewers a large volume of challenging, comprehensible input. Captioned videos also provide a rich source of simulated social interactions; captioning is not distracting during language learning. I agree that the technique of combining text and sound can lead learners to focus consciously on word form, particularly on unfamiliar technical terms or proper names. However, this integration may also help learners understand contextual cues within videos. Such cues can capture learners' attention and help them tease out word meaning, similar to the "noticing" reaction described by Schmidt (1990). Learners who notice contextual clues in language input should be able to process and encode the message even if it exceeds their current comprehension competency. Learners with captions can also cope better with longer stretches of text at once, enabling them to process messages more effectively in longer stretches of speech. The presence of captions has been described as helping learners develop a "chunking ability" in reading and listening (Vanderplank, 2016b, p. 53), which can promote gradual and conscious learning.

Multimedia Learning Theory

Mayer (2001) proposed a multimedia learning theory. According to this theory, multimedia learning decreases learners' extraneous cognitive load and guides their attention toward germane materials, thereby increasing schema related to cognitive load. Focusing on germane materials constitutes the basis for effective learning. This theoretical conceptualization is based on three main assumptions: (1) the dual-channel assumption (i.e., there should be two separate channels [auditory and visual] for information processing); (2) the limited capacity assumption (i.e., each channel has a limited channel capacity); and (3) the active processing assumption (i.e., learning becomes meaningful because multimedia helps learners filter, select, organize, and integrate information). This theory is also called the "multimedia principle," which claims that "people learn more deeply from words and pictures than from words alone" (Mayer, 2001, p. 47). Mayer also discussed the role of three memory stores, namely sensory memory (i.e., a function of receiving stimuli and storing it within a short time), working memory (i.e., a function of processing information to create mental schema), and long-term memory (i.e., one's repository of learned information). Figure 2.1 depicts how memory works according to Mayer's (2009) cognitive theory of multimedia learning. It illustrates five forms of representation of words and pictures that occur as information is processed via memory. The first form refers to words and pictures in the multimedia presentation itself. The second form includes ears and eyes in sensory memory. The third form contains the sounds and images in working memory. The fourth form consists of the verbal and pictorial models also belonging to working memory. The fifth form contains prior knowledge stored in long-term memory.

Learners' brains do not interpret a multimedia presentation of words, pictures, and auditory information in a mutually exclusive fashion. Learners, with support from multimedia learning, instead select and organize elements to produce logical mental constructs.

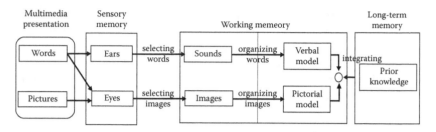

Figure 2.1 Mayer's (2009) Cognitive Theory of Multimedia Learning.

Given this theory, multimedia learning provides coherent verbal and pictorial information. This input guides learners to select appropriate words and images and lowers the load on a single processing channel. Information is stored in schemas. Along with the progression of learning, schemas become increasingly sophisticated and are then developed and transferred from controlled to automatic processing. As argued by Plass and Jones (2005), the combination of verbal and nonverbal input may prompt learners to perceive, comprehend, subsume, and merge new information within their mental system. Learners need visual and textual aids to construct stronger meaning representations for retrieval of language input.

Baddeley's Model of Working Memory

Under Baddeley's (1986) model, the central executive is a vital component of working memory. The central executive is responsible for controlling the system and solving problems. It can also transfer storage tasks and the flow of information to its slave systems, the visuospatial sketchpad and the phonological loop, which are the two subcomponent systems of working memory. The central executive thus has the capacity for tasks that demand an information processing load. The visuospatial sketchpad is responsible for maintaining and manipulating visual images, while the phonological loop is intended for the storing and rehearsal of verbal information. The phonological loop also plays an important function in enhancing language learning by inserting a new word into working memory. Both slave systems function as short-term storage centers. Baddeley (2000) later proposed the addition of a third subsystem, the episodic buffer, which is responsible for integrating multiple sources of information from other systems. This revised model is illustrated in Figure 2.2.

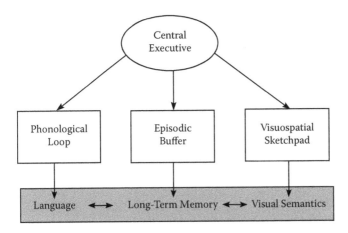

Figure 2.2 Second Working Memory Model (Baddeley, 2000).

Considerable evidence has emerged to support the second working memory model. Empirical data have also pointed to additional subcomponents within slave-specific-domain working memory systems. For example, Baddeley, Allen, and Hitch (2011) developed the latest model (Figure 2.3), which contains previously missing sensory modalities and highlights the importance of the episodic buffer in integrating modalities. Different from the previous model, the central executive exclusively coordinates the episodic buffer and demonstrates no connections between the central executive and other subsystems. The episodic buffer integrates information and coordinates directly with the slave subsystems to execute demands from the central executive.

Dual-coding Theory

Paivio (1986, 2007) hypothesized dual-coding theory, based on which there are two ways an individual can expand upon learned materials: verbal associations and visual imagery. Visual and verbal forms of information are processed differently, and individuals create separate representations for information processed in each channel. The ability to code a stimulus in two ways (e.g., a word and a picture for "table") increases one's chance of remembering that item compared to a situation in which the stimulus is only coded in one way (Sternberg, 2003). Danan (1992) linked dual-coding theory to the use

24 *Captioned Videos*

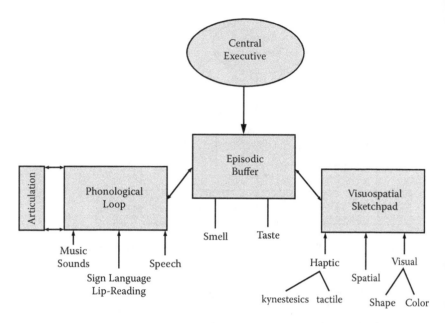

Figure 2.3 The Latest Model of Working Memory (Baddeley et al., 2011).

of captions for language learning. Specifically, information simultaneously encoded verbally and nonverbally in captioned videos is more likely to be stored in memory than a single and separate information processing channel of either verbal information processing (e.g., speech) or nonverbal information processing (e.g., visual images). This argument implies the value of adding nonverbal input to videos to enhance young learners' ability to discern unknown words (Teng, 2019a). In this respect, I further argued that captioned videos can serve as a worthwhile scaffold for young students learning English as a second language (ESL). These videos can promote vocabulary learning by providing verbal and nonverbal information simultaneously (i.e., speech accompanied by dynamic visual content). The process involved in watching captioned videos does not appear to be overwhelming in terms of bimodal input but instead acts as a support, helping learners synthesize multiple representations of the same information. This phenomenon was explained through Paivio's (1986) early "dual-coding theory," wherein memory purportedly consists of one verbal and one visual system that can be activated independently while interconnections between the systems allow for dual coding of information. Within this connection, the text presented in captioned videos may serve to promote a synopsis of dynamic speech (Vanderplank, 1993).

According to the dual-coding theory, if the information is presented in picture- and language-like forms, then learners are more likely to build an elaborate coding system containing more than one route to recall information. They are also more likely to recognize, process, and store extra information in both systems rather than in just one. Finally, they should store information in the system that corresponds best to a given type of information (i.e., verbal or imagery). Hence, audiovisual input should facilitate learning better than audio-only treatment.

Cognitive Load Theory

According to cognitive load theory, learners' working memory is limited. However, working memory can be maximized by mixing auditory and visual modes of presentation as proposed by the dual-coding theory described above. Learners' cognitive load can take one of three forms: (1) intrinsic (i.e., demands placed upon a learner by the intrinsic quality of information being learned); (2) extraneous (i.e., demands placed upon learners by the teacher or instructions they are asked to follow); or (3) germane (i.e., a type of cognitive load produced by the construction of schemas and considered desirable, as it facilitates the acquisition of new skills and other information). Due to the modality effect (Mayer, 2001), the audiovisual presentation of information (i.e., combined audio and text) allows for better use of cognitive resources. The split-attention effect further suggests that presenting disparate sources of information in the same modality may lead learners to divide their attention, creating a heavy cognitive processing load and fewer resources available for learning. By contrast, presenting information in two different modalities (e.g., auditory and visual) reduces this cognitive load and affords learners multiple means of information processing, storage, and retrieval.

Hence, the dual-coding theory provides knowledge about how information is processed via two cognitive systems. Cognitive load theory implies that working memory can be maximized through a dual presentation of information because such a presentation provides multiple means of processing, storage, and retrieval. Learners' cognitive load typically increases when they face unnecessary demands, including distractions (e.g., unfamiliar terms or proper names), while watching videos or programs. When their cognitive load is managed well, students can learn new skills more easily than when a high cognitive load interferes with memory. Learners develop memories when auditory and visual information can be processed (or rehearsed) to a greater degree. Captions thus help reduce cognitive load in a multimedia learning environment and strengthen learners' memory for new language input.

Models for Understanding Language Learning From Captioned Viewing

Learning a language through captioned viewing may be difficult. Vanderplank (2016b) proposed two models to identify challenges in teaching and learning a language. These models are an attempt to capture the factors that influence language learning. The first model (Figure 2.4) identifies attention-related factors, which determine whether a video viewer-learner can exert concerted effort when watching a video or program to gain linguistic competence. These factors are also tied to learners' perceived self-efficacy for video viewing; a lack of self-efficacy influences learners' capacity to comprehend language while viewing videos. In Figure 2.4, attention, including selection factors (e.g., learners' motivation and attitude) and grading factors (e.g., current knowledge, current skill level in English, language/information load, mode of presentation, and program length), affect learners' ability to absorb comprehensible input and internalize language during intake. According to this model, whether learners are conscious of their language learning affects the outcomes of captioned video viewing experiences.

However, the attention factors proposed by Vanderplank (2016b) are not sufficient to capture what learners will likely do when presented with extensive comprehensible input and with the complex process of absorbing language. Vanderplank (2016b) therefore refined the model (Figure 2.5).

Figure 2.5 shows that a learner needs conscious, systematic, and reflective attention when presented with extensive comprehensible input. Subsequent steps include adaptation and adoption, which are part of "taking out" (i.e., learning from audiovisual input). Learners first need to adapt to appropriate spoken or written language before they can adopt it; however, adopting someone else's language is not equal to the process of "taking in" (i.e., "being absorbed or assimilated into one's linguistic competence" (Vanderplank, 1990, p. 229).

The refined model in Figure 2.5 does not provide loops within the selection and grading process for learners to enact choice or control.

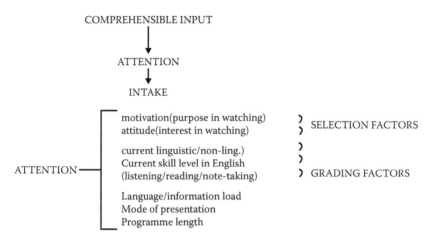

Figure 2.4 Model of Attention With Selection and Grading Factors (Vanderplank, 2016b, p. 63).

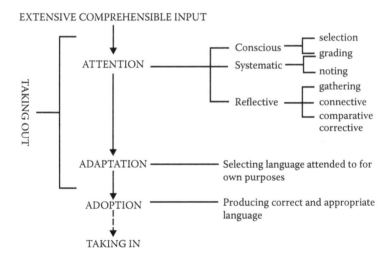

Figure 2.5 Model of "Paying Attention to the Words" (Vanderplank, 2016b, p. 64).

28 *Captioned Videos*

It also fails to capture the perceptual aspects of captioned viewing. To overcome these limitations, Vanderplank (2016b) proposed a cognitive-affective model (Figure 2.6).

The model in Figure 2.6 aims to identify complex processes and illustrate what is needed for learners to learn actively when watching captioned material. I concur with Vanderplank (2016b) that language learning through captioned videos is inherently challenging, as this process involves many variables. In the cognitive-affective model in Figure 2.6, attention plays a significant role. Attention is part of the process rather than the end. Like the model in Figure 2.5, attention and adaptation are included in "taking out." The difference between these two models is the new boxes that have been added to the attention and adaptation stages. The highly elaborate processes in the attention and adaptation stages consider learners' motivation, attitude, and other affective factors. The rationale behind this model is that viewing an available captioned program does not guarantee automatic taking out of the target language. Motivation and attitude

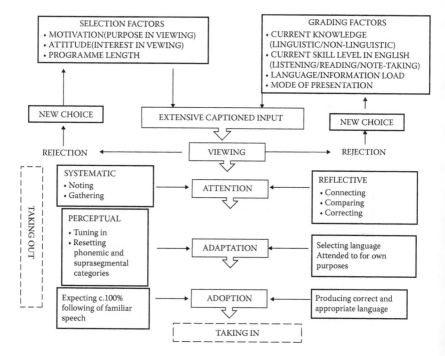

Figure 2.6 A Cognitive-affective Model of Language Learning Through Captioned Viewing (Vanderplank, 2016b, p. 240).

affect one's level of engagement with the program. When it comes to EFL viewers, achieving conscious, systematic, and reflective attention to take out the target language requires much more to be done.

In a recent study (Teng, 2019a), I observed 257 students in Grade 6 (131 boys and 126 girls) from six primary schools in Hong Kong. Results showed that primary school ESL learners can indeed learn new words by watching a video in English with full captions. In addition, the frequency of word occurrence may augment incidental vocabulary learning. When words were encountered three times in the full captioning condition, learners demonstrated better learning outcomes. Based on these findings, I proposed a new model (Figure 2.7) to delineate the dual-modal presentation technique for enhancing the form-meaning link of new words learned from captioned videos.

In this model, it is assumed that captioned videos may provide opportunities for learners to carry out cognitive coordination of the

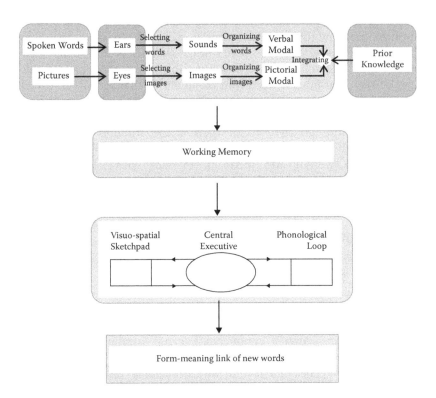

Figure 2.7 Dual Model Representation of Facilitating a Form-Meaning Link of New Words (Teng, 2019a).

two perceptual domains (i.e., auditory and visual components) because the information presented in each modality is insufficient for meaning determination. Enacting this dual-modal representation (specifically integrating verbal modal input from the ears and pictorial modal input from the eyes) while interacting with prior knowledge may help learners activate working memory to establish a form-meaning link for new words. Learners' working memory, which functions as the central executive, coordinates information retrieved from the two storage subsystems of the visuospatial sketchpad and phonological loop. The coordination of this information facilitates the development of a form-meaning link for new words.

The benefits of using captioned videos in incidental vocabulary learning can also be explained through Baddeley's (1986) working memory model, in which the use of two perceptual domains (i.e., a visual and verbal task) does not cause one to interfere with the other. The coordination of verbal associations and visual imagery is assumed to be governed by (a) the central executive, which controls the flow of information; and (b) the episodic buffer, a limited capacity system that provides temporary information storage (Baddeley, 2000). In other words, while learners receive imagery information, they may be able to derive verbal information from the auditory channel, supporting a dual-modal presentation technique (Xu et al. 2008). In other words, coding a stimulus (in this case, vocabulary) in two distinct ways promotes more effective recall than if the stimulus were coded through either representation alone. Two forms of mental representation, verbal and pictorial, interact with learners' prior knowledge and form an enhanced level of working memory available for processing concrete information related to new words.

Concluding Remarks

Language learning has become more accessible because of multimedia technology. Captions can activate both coding systems of words and pictures. In line with the dual-coding theory, the cues associated with the message increase when combining pictures and messages. Hence, the use of captions can trigger multi-sensory processing. Through such input sources, learners' content comprehension and vocabulary acquisition may be enhanced.

Captions may be an effective way of helping ESL teaching and learning. ESL programs could consider the integration of captioned videos and programs into the curricula to assist students' language learning. As discussed in this chapter, captioning is an innovative and promising approach to enhancing students' L2 learning. Despite the benefits, further exploration into the potential of captioned videos on L2 teaching and learning is still needed.

In conclusion, it is essential to consider captioned programs in view of the communicative objectives of the curriculum. Interpreted from multimedia learning theory, captions afford learners with opportunities to view and learn words in a comprehensible, meaningful, and stimulating context. Learners benefit from the combination of visual and auditory input. Construed from input hypothesis and cognitive load theory, the use of visual, graphic and aural cues through captioned videos can reduce students' cognitive load when viewing programs. Their enhanced motivation and interest for learning reduce their learning anxiety and lower their negative feelings such as lack of confidence. The lack of motivation and confidence may hinder and obstruct their language learning (Krashen, 1989). Hence, presenting verbal and visual learning materials is encouraging and can make the learning condition more authentic, lively, and interesting to the students.

References

Baddeley, A. D. (1986). *Working memory*. New York: Oxford University Press.
Baddeley, A. (2000). The episodic buffer: A new component of working memory? *Trends in Cognitive Sciences*, 4(11), 417–423.
Baddeley, A. D., Allen, R. J., & Hitch, G. J. (2011). Binding in visual working memory: The role of the episodic buffer. *Neuropsychologia*, 49(1), 1393–1400.
Danan, M. (1992). Reversed subtitling and dual coding theory: New directions for foreign language instruction. *Language Learning*, 42(4), 497–527.
Danan, M. (2004). Captioning and subtitling: Undervalued language learning strategies. *Meta: Translators' Journal*, 49(1), 67–77.
Diao, Y., Chandler, P., & Sweller, J. (2007). The effect of written text on comprehension of spoken English as a foreign language. *American Journal of Psychology*, 120(1), 237–261.
Fletcher, J. D., & Tobias, S. (2005). The multimedia principle. In Mayer, R. E. (Ed.), *The Cambridge Handbook of Multimedia Learning* (pp. 117–133). Cambridge University Press: Cambridge.
Koolstra, C. M., & Beentjes, J. W. (1999). Children's vocabulary acquisition in a foreign language through watching subtitled television programs at home. *Educational Technology Research & Development*, 47(1), 51–60.
Krashen, S. D. (1989). We acquire vocabulary and spelling by reading: Additional evidence for the input hypothesis. *The Modern Language Journal*, 73(4), 440–464.
Latifi, M., Mobalegh, A., & Mohammadi, E. (2011). Movie subtitles and the improvement of listening comprehension ability: Does it help? *The Journal of Language Teaching and Learning*, 1(2), 18–29.

Jelani, N., & Boers, F. (2018). Examining incidental vocabulary acquisition from captioned video. Does test modality matter? *ITL - International Journal of Applied Linguistics, 169*(1), 169–190.

Mayer, R. E. (2001). *Multimedia learning*. Cambridge: Cambridge University Press.

Mayer, R. E. (2009). *Multimedia learning* (2nd). Cambridge: Cambridge University Press.

Montero Perez, M., Peters, E., Clarebout, G., & Desmet, P. (2014). Effects of captioning on video comprehension and incidental vocabulary learning. *Language Learning & Technology, 18*(1), 118–141.

Montero Perez, M., Peters, E., & Desmet, P. (2015). Enhancing vocabulary learning through captioned video: An eye-tracking study. *The Modern Language Journal, 99*(2), 308–328.

Montero Perez, M. M., Peters, E., & Desmet, P. (2018). Vocabulary learning through viewing video: The effect of two enhancement techniques. *Computer Assisted Language Learning, 31(1)*, 1–26.

Montero Perez, M., Van Den Noortgate, W., & Desmet, P. (2013). Captioned video for L2 listening and vocabulary learning: A meta-analysis. *System, 41*(3), 720–739.

Muñoz, C. (2017) The role of age and proficiency in subtitle reading. An eye-tracking study, *System, 67 (1)*, 77–86.

Paivio, A. (1986). *Mental representation: A dual-coding approach*. New York: Oxford University Press.

Paivio, A. (2007). *Mind and its evolution: A dual coding theoretical approach*. Mahwah, NJ: Erlbaum.

Peters, E., Heynen, E., & Puimège, E. (2016). Learning vocabulary through audiovisual input: The differential effect of L1 subtitles and captions. *System, 63*(1), 134–148.

Peters, E., & Webb, S. (2018). Incidental vocabulary acquisition through viewing L2 television and factors that affect learning. *Studies in Second Language Acquisition, 40*(3), 551–577.

Plass, J. L. & Jones, L. C. (2005). *Multimedia learning in second language acquisition*. In R. E. Mayer (Ed.), *The Cambridge handbook of multimedia learning* (pp. 467–488). New York, NY, US: Cambridge University Press.

Reynolds, B. L., & Teng, F. (2020). *Vocabulary Bridge-Building: A book review of Norbert Schmitt (2010), I. S. Paul Nation & Stuart Webb (2011), and Paul Meara & Imma Miralpeix (2016)*, Applied Linguistics, 41(4), 612–617 https://doi.org/10.1093/applin/amy021.

Rodgers, M. (2013). *English language learning through viewing television: An investigation of comprehension, incidental vocabulary acquisition, lexical coverage, attitudes and captions*. Unpublished doctoral dissertation, New Zealand: Victoria University of Wellington.

Rott, S. (2007). The effect of frequency of input-enhancements on word learning and text comprehension. *Language Learning, 57*(1), 165–199.

Schmidt, R. W. (1990). The role of consciousness in second language learning. *Applied Linguistics, 11*(2), 129–158.

Sternberg, R. J. (2003). *Cognitive theory* (3rd ed.). Belmont, CA: Thomson Wadsworth.

Sydorenko, T. (2010). Modality of input and vocabulary acquisition. *Language Learning & Technology, 14,* 50–73.

Swain, M., & Lapkin, S. (2001). *Researching pedagogic tasks.* England: Pearson Education Limited.

Taylor, G. (2005). Perceived processing strategies of students watching captioned video. *Foreign Language Annals, 38*(3), 422–427.

Teng, F. (2017). Flipping the classroom and tertiary level EFL students' academic performance and satisfaction. *The Journal of Asia TEFL, 14*(4), 605–620.

Teng, F. (2018). Incidental vocabulary acquisition from reading-only and reading-while-listening: A multi-dimensional approach. *Innovation in Language Learning and Teaching, 12*(3), 274–288.

Teng, F. (2019a). Incidental vocabulary learning for primary school students: The effects of L2 caption type and word exposure frequency. *The Australian Educational Researcher, 46*(1), 113–136.

Teng, F. (2019b). Retention of new words learned incidentally from reading: Word exposure frequency, L1 marginal glosses, and their combination. *Language Teaching Research.* https://journals.sagepub.com/doi/10.1177/1362168819829026.

Teng, F., & Reynolds, B. L. (2019). Effects of individual and group metacognitive prompts on EFL reading comprehension and incidental vocabulary learning. *PLOS One.* https://journals.plos.org/plosone/article?id=10.1371/journal.pone.0215902.

Vanderplank, R. (1988). The value of teletext sub-titles in language learning. *ELT Journal, 42*(4), 272–281.

Vanderplank, R. (1990). Paying attention to the words: Practical and theoretical problems in watching television programmes with uni-lingual (CEEFAX) sub-titles. *System, 18*(2), 221–234.

Vanderplank, R. (1993). A very verbal medium: Language learning through closed captions. *TESOL Journal, 3*(1), 10–14.

Vanderplank, R. (2016a). 'Effects of' and 'effects with' captions: How exactly does watching a TV programme with same-language subtitles make a difference to language learners? *Language Teaching, 49*(2), 235–250.

Vanderplank, R. (2016b). *Captioned media in foreign language learning and teaching: Subtitles for the deaf and hard-of-hearing as tools for language learning.* Oxford: Palgrave Macmillan.

Webb, S., & Chang, A. C.-S. (2015). Second language vocabulary learning through extensive reading: How does frequency and distribution of occurrence affect learning? *Language Teaching Research, 19*(6), 667–686.

Webb, S., & Nation, I. S. P. (2017). *How vocabulary is learned.* Oxford: Oxford University Press.

Winke, P., Gass, S. M., & Sydorenko, T. (2010). The effects of captioning videos used for foreign language listening activities. *Language Learning & Technology, 14*(1), 66–87.

Winke, P., Gass, S., & Sydorenko, T. (2013). Factors influencing the use of captions by foreign language learners: An eye-tracking study. *The Modern Language Journal, 97*(1), 254–275.

Xu, S., Fang, X. W., Brzezinski, J., & Chan, S. (2008). Development of a dual-modal presentation of texts for small screens. *International Journal of Human-Computer Interaction, 24*(8), 776–793.

3 Language Learning and Incidental Vocabulary Acquisition From Captioned Videos
Advantages and Disadvantages

We live in a global society dominated by technology. With ever-growing demands to enhance education, the call to incorporate technology into ESL teaching and learning has arisen. Integrating video technology into classroom instruction is essential to students' language learning. Captioning is not an innovative technology, but it offers contextual language support to facilitate language teaching and learning. Through captions, learners can see words, read them, hear them spoken, and view them within a particular context along with action on the TV screen. As a result, learners can enjoy a rich learning environment. This simultaneous audio and written visual context can aid comprehension of complicated terminology or items.

Incidentally, online video-sharing sites are becoming increasingly popular in the educational domain. Captions offer tremendous opportunities for teachers to enhance content comprehension. Three popular resources that can be used for pedagogical purposes are YouTube, Netflix, and Google Videos. Other open resources for educational purposes (e.g., TeacherTube and Academic Earth free courses) are also receiving more attention. Free online video downloaders (e.g., Vixy.net and KeepVid) can convert online videos into multimedia formats, promoting the use of flipped classrooms. Teachers can use specific online programs (i.e., iMovie or Adobe Premiere) to generate on-screen text for videos. With advances in technology and user-friendly interfaces, teachers can harness these expanding open-source video tools for language teaching. While I argue for the advantages of captions in ESL learning, using captioned videos/programs for language teaching and learning also carries some disadvantages.

Benefits of Captions

Captioning is the most common form of assistive technology for the deaf; it is a synchronized textual alternative to audio. Captions may be open or closed. Open captions, like subtitles, refer to the text displayed as part of a TV program and commonly accessible through a decoder. Closed captions can be turned on and off. Closed captions include dialogue and descriptions of other relevant parts of a program's soundtrack (e.g., background noises, phones ringing, and other audio cues). Closed captions are only displayed when activated by the viewer and generally appear at the bottom of the TV screen. Despite being initially intended for the deaf and hard of hearing, captions are increasingly being used as a tool to learn a second or foreign language.

Information can only be held in short-term memory for a few seconds before deterioration. For information to be assimilated into long-term memory, learner effort is required. However, research has shown that the auditory presentation of information can yield better retention (Plass & Jones, 2005). Compared to audio information, visual information in multimedia formats (e.g., video) is often available for more extended periods. Learners may then have a longer time to assimilate the presented information. Audiovisual input also strengthens a viewer's understanding and perception of a given presentation. Generally, captions can help individuals assimilate information into memory.

Perceived Usefulness of Captions

Most relevant studies have focused on the benefits of captions by measuring post-intervention listening (Winke, Gass, & Sydorenko, 2010) and vocabulary learning performance (Montero Perez, Peters, Clarebout, & Desmet, 2014). However, how learners perceive the usefulness of captioning is similarly essential to consider. Based on Pujolà's (2002) assertions, listening proficiency is associated with learners' perceptions of transcripts and subtitles. Learners with higher ability were found to perceive and use captions more "as a backup to their listening activity". In contrast, other learners considered them "a more necessary tool in their understanding of the authentic aural input" (p. 254). In addition to their linguistic levels, learners' perceptions and beliefs about the nature of a task, and how learners approach it also appear to influence their learning performance. Hence, learners' perceptions might affect their use of captioned videos.

Studies have indicated that presenting a video with audio and captions can benefit vocabulary learning. One caveat is that learners might not focus on audio when they have captions at their disposal. Winke et al. (2010) observed that learners perceived captions as a "crutch" (p. 81), as learners were required to match what they heard with the corresponding visualization in the captions. In Vanderplank's (1988) study, captioning was a "mediating device" (p. 280). Park (2004) found that due to different proficiency levels, learners' attitudes toward keyword captions varied. For example, learners at a high-intermediate level reacted positively to captions while those at intermediate and low-intermediate levels found captions distracting.

One reason why learners might not focus on audio when watching captioned video is that the three types of stimuli—visual images, text, and audio—divert learners' attention. Due to the learners' limited attentional capacity, they must selectively attend to different modalities (Wickens, 2007). When learners attempt to focus on all three modalities, cognitive overload may follow. Such overload is attributed to the limits of working memory (Baddeley, 1992). According to Sweller's (2005) cognitive load theory, redundant material hinders learners' information processing, and learning.

Additionally, using three modes of presentation (i.e., video, audio, and on-screen text) may be more beneficial for language learning than only two ways (i.e., video and audio). But do second or foreign language learners differ from native speakers in how they focus on these three types of input? Some may switch between images and captions. Others may not pay much attention to visual images but instead concentrate on captions because some pictures may not carry useful information. Still, others may not be able to process audio as well as captions. However, over time, learners can develop strategies for processing audiovisual input. More studies are needed to understand how learners perceive and process captioned videos. One factor that may affect learners' engagement and perceptions of captioned videos is language proficiency.

Levels of Language Proficiency and Captioned Video Learning

This chapter introduces many vital factors. For example, learners' language proficiency is key to the perceived value of captioned programs for EFL learning. I investigated 223 university EFL students who took a listening and reading comprehension test modeled after the International English Language Testing System. After taking the test, participants watched a series of captioned videos that included words with which they were unfamiliar. After watching the videos, they took a test that measured their video content comprehension. Table 3.1 presents the correlations among these tests.

As illustrated in Table 3.1, EFL students' listening and reading comprehension tests were each significantly correlated with captioned-video comprehension ($p < .01$). Their listening proficiency produced a correlation of .758, indicating a strong relationship between listening proficiency and the quality of captioned-video comprehension. Reading comprehension displayed a slightly lower correlation of .753, but no statistically significant difference was observed in the strength with which these two variables correlated with captioned-video comprehension. Therefore, based on the analysis, the two dimensions of English language proficiency (i.e., listening and reading comprehension) should be regarded as having equally strong associations with video comprehension. Multiple regression analysis (Table 3.2) and the bootstrapping process showed that listening and reading comprehension significantly affected students' ability to comprehend captioned videos.

The benefits of full scripts on videos influenced learners' reading skills. Unsurprisingly, learners with more advanced English levels appeared to benefit from textual support, as shown in one of my studies (Teng, 2019a). Although I did not arrange a writing and speaking proficiency test for these learners, their language proficiency appeared to contribute substantially to their comprehension of captioned videos. Learners below the intermediate level and some slow learners may have found it challenging to comprehend captioned videos. The chosen videos focused on TV news programs. More attention should be given to the selection and grading aspects of these videos, as many programs that include far fewer words per minute than TV news programs are available.

Table 3.1 Pearson Correlations Among Listening and Reading Proficiency and Captioned Video Comprehension ($n = 223$)

		Captioned Video Comprehension	Listening Comprehension
Pearson Correlation	Listening proficiency	0.758	–
	Reading proficiency	0.753	0.80**

Note
**indicates that the result is significant at $p < 0.01$ (two-tailed).

Table 3.2 Multiple Analysis Results

Model	Unstandardized Coefficients		Standardized Coefficients	t	Sig.	Correlations		
	B	Std. Error	Beta			Zero-order	Partial	Part
1 (Constant)	2.205	0.097		22.831	0.000			
Listening comprehension	1.938	0.138	0.512	14.029	0.000	0.658	0.735	0.363
Reading comprehension	1.932	0.137	0.510	14.147	0.000	0.653	0.738	0.366

Perceived Advantage of Captions

I also invited the 223 students to complete a survey regarding how they perceived the use of captions. I received 150 responses. Survey respondents were asked to check all options applied to them from a predetermined list regarding why they used captions. Respondents were also given the option to choose "other" and describe alternative reasons. The results appear in Figure 3.1.

Most learners seemed to agree that understanding information and learning vocabulary are the two main benefits of captioned videos. Content comprehension was the next most frequently chosen benefit, followed by adapting to the spoken speed, understanding the plot, retaining information, helping with reading and writing, and understanding odd accents. Apart from "other," the smallest proportion of learners selected "understanding cultural knowledge" as a benefit.

I also interviewed 20 learners and found that, although captions were initially intended for those who are deaf and hard of hearing, captions can also be an effective means of accessing foreign-language TV programs and films that would otherwise be nearly incomprehensible to EFL learners who need assistance with language learning. While many TV programs are available to EFL learners, a lack of captions may prevent them from gaining a meaningful sense of

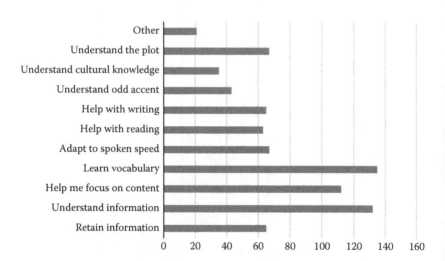

Figure 3.1 Learners' Perceived Benefits of Using Captioned Videos.

the content. When viewing videos, learners who do not have access to a full script may not fully understand the content. This type of interface may be based on rough phonetic matching. Captions function as a tool for providing the recognizable and intelligible script. Captions can help learners fill in the missing parts of the speech they have heard, thus making the interface of sound and perception more accurate. Watching captioned videos is not the same as basic reading or listening activities; it implies hearing sounds while reading text and viewing pictures. The different channels created by captioned videos lead to the unconscious integration of the senses. As learners continue to try to match the sound with text and monitor their internal matching of input from these channels, captions may produce long-term improvements in retention and recall.

A group of students who attended class instruction focusing on captioned videos provided positive feedback about the experience, which I classified into six themes.

Positive Flipped Classroom Experiences Through Using Videos

Most interviewees (n = 15) revealed they had not participated in flipped teaching using captioned videos before, and many (n = 12) expressed interest in engaging in this form of experiential learning because they found captions helpful for learning material beyond textbooks. They believed that using videos in a flipped classroom would become a future trend, as reflected in the following excerpts:

> *Learning English from textbooks cannot help us pick up the conversational stuff. The captioned videos can help us understand conversation better, particularly for those of us who are not native English speakers.* (Interviewee 3)

> *It is quite interesting to watch the teachers and fellows acting out. It really helps me get the meaning of some difficult words. Captions help a lot because they are refreshing.* (Interviewee 8)

Enhanced Content Comprehension

Eighteen students discussed how captioned videos influenced their content understanding. The following quotes indicate how viewing captions helped learners develop language comprehension:

> Sometimes when you are lost in the plot, it gives you a hint. I'd guess that the videos help me understand the new words, thus improving my comprehension of the content. (Interviewee 4)

Learners also stressed why captions could help them understand more content. For example, a lack of proficiency in understanding spoken speech led some students to realize the benefits of captions in language learning:

> I think without captions, it would be very difficult for me to understand the video content. I was not so familiar with the sounds and pronunciation. Sometimes the speakers talked so fast. (Interviewee 6)

> I found captions particularly useful for understanding some important words. For example, the captions helped me understand the contextual clues surrounding a new word. If I didn't understand the key words, I may stop watching that video. (Interviewee 5)

Without captions, learners often tended to guess the meaning of words; however, they lacked confidence. Some noted that they could only guess roughly half the words, while some stated they could guess more:

> I think without captions, I had to make a guess for most of the words. I am not sure whether I can make a reliable estimate, maybe 60%. (Interviewee 9)

Enhanced Language Skills

About two-thirds of learners reported that their language skills, including accents, vocabulary, listening, speaking, reading, and writing, were improved after the flipped class using captioned videos:

> I believe this flipped classroom experience has enhanced my listening comprehension. I think I understood more because of the captions. Over each week, I have been able to pick up more words. If we don't have captioned videos, like in our traditional classroom, we just listen, and then we can't figure out what the teacher said. (Interviewee 1)

I think one thing that I learned from the captioned videos was that I could put the words together in a sentence. Learning vocabulary is not just through reciting. You need some pictures or actions to stimulate your understanding and use of the words. (Interviewee 5)

I would say for speaking, captioned videos definitely help because you could use what you have learned in the videos to talk to someone. (Interviewee 4)

In addition, captions enhanced learners' reading and writing performance. For example, understanding text structures was one benefit the participants cited frequently. Text structures in audiovisual input may have also helped participants notice the main idea and details of material:

Thanks to captions, I improved my reading and writing. When I focused on the words and content, I found myself gradually improving my reading and writing ability. I would reflect on how to use the text structure in my reading and writing. The captions helped me understand more about movie plots. (Interviewee 11)

Participants also mentioned that captions enhanced other learning aspects, such as accents. When TV programs or videos sometimes contained unfamiliar accents, participants appreciated having captions, which made the accents easier to understand:

With the help of captions, I became less scared of an unfamiliar foreign accent. Some English was spoken by Indian people. It was so difficult for me to understand it without captions. (Interviewee 13)

The above quote highlights some challenges in understanding Indian English. The term "scared" described this learner's experience when listening to an "unfamiliar foreign accent." Other participants also mentioned that captioned videos helped them adapt to the talking speed as non-native English speakers.

Enhanced Understanding of Cultural Knowledge and Language Context

The following quotes highlight the advantages of captions in helping learners understand cultural knowledge:

> *I think the captions helped me to understand some cultural knowledge. Without captions, I might have ignored some cultural issues.* (Interviewee 14)

Other participants mentioned the benefits of captions in becoming familiar with "characters," "dialogue," "detailed information," and "rapid speaking speed." These factors were all important for "retaining key information," as one participant mentioned:

> *With captions, I could understand more about the characters, and the complicated dialogue, detailed information, and rapid speaking speed of native speakers. Captions helped me retain key information.* (Interviewee 15)

In particular, one learner recalled that the language context enriched their understanding, noting that captions represented an effective way to experience natural language contexts to which non-native English speakers would otherwise not be exposed in everyday life:

> *Language learning needs a context. What I mean is we don't have peers to speak English with us. In daily life, we don't have English conversation. You may just be able to listen to Chinese conversation. There is not a lot of exposure to English conversation input. Captioned videos are a good way to listen to English conversation .* (Interviewee 16)

Enhanced Confidence in Language Learning

Participants also mentioned emotional aspects such as confidence. Learning English as a foreign language—especially in a context where English input is insufficient—can be especially difficult. Learners often struggle with low self-confidence, whereas captions may help to enhance one's confidence:

> *I think captions made me become more confident, and the video-watching experiences less tiring. I realized the need to take notes and organize information from captions.* (Interviewee 2)

> *I am pretty sure I have gained some confidence in listening comprehension as I watched programs with the support of captions.* (Interviewee 6)

I think I became less dependent on the captions. The dialogue in the videos seemed less rapid than before because I adapted to the speed of the speakers. I became more confident. (Interviewee 8)

In the above comments, Interviewee 2 mentioned that the confidence he gained from captions kept him from becoming bored while watching TV programs. Interviewee 6 noted greater confidence in his listening comprehension. Interviewee 8 discussed her growing confidence in adapting to the rate of speakers' speech. Confidence is fundamental to language learning, serving as a catalyst for the process and enjoyment of language learning. Motivation is also a psychological aspect of language learning. Enhanced confidence in language learning is a stimulus for language learners, and captioning is an effective technique to boost their confidence in becoming more attuned to language input.

Incorporating Captioned Videos into the Curriculum

Learners shared positive impressions of using captioned videos and identified related strengths and weaknesses. The learners also recommended incorporating captioned videos into curriculum design and development. They further suggested integrating video sessions to accommodate ESL learners' needs:

I think captioned videos should be more widely used in our curriculum. We could have more class activities after watching the captioned videos. I thought they were good. We cannot just rely on our textbooks. (Interviewee 11)

I think captioned videos could be used more in future curricula. Well, we can read well and understand well through textbooks. But the speed is very slow. In daily life, people do not speak like that. To hear and understand people speak at a normal speed, we surely need more captioned videos. (Interviewee 6)

Perceived Disadvantage in Captions

Some learners shared constructive criticism regarding the use of captions. Survey respondents were asked to check all options that applied to them from a predetermined list regarding why they used captions.

Respondents could also choose "other" and describe an alternative reason. The results are shown in Figure 3.2.

Learners seemed to express anxiety about their limited listening skills and language proficiency, representing the main reasons why the learners felt they had missed the benefits of captions. Other reasons included speakers' unusual accents, inability to process audiovisual input, a fast rate of speech, and distractions due to captions. These reasons were also reported in Vanderplank (2016). A few learners noted disadvantages related to topic-based and cultural unfamiliarity.

I analyzed 20 learners' interview responses, as well. Some learners noted related disadvantages in language learning. A possible argument based on data analysis is that captions distracted learners because they became dependent on the captions and then found it challenging to watch English-language programs without text support:

> *I am a Chinese speaker with a poor English. With captions, you look at it but sometimes you just pay attention to the text on the video. When you watch the video, you just end up reading all the words.* (Interviewee 4).

Other participants shared negative comments regarding their use of captions. Factors included the film/program genre, amount or quality of speech, listening proficiency, and language proficiency:

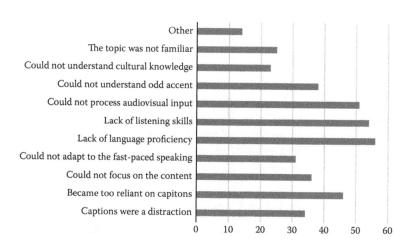

Figure 3.2 Learners' Perceived Disadvantages of Viewing Captions.

Sometimes I think captions were a distraction for me because when I focused on them, then I forgot the sound and the picture. Captions actually required too much cognitive load. There were instances when I had to concentrate solely on reading the captions. I still could not understand anything because my English proficiency is not good. (Interviewee 2)

I think we should focus more on reading and writing. That is the difficult part in language learning. The native speakers speak too fast in the video. You can't learn anything from the video. (Interviewee 5)

Data showed that one reason captions may distract learners is individuals' lack of English proficiency:

The accessibility to the language provided by the captions might have influenced my effort at video watching because I became more dependent on the captions. I always stopped and rewatched some parts of the video. The speaker was so fast, I could not focus on the meaning within a strict time limit. (Interviewee 6)

In the above quote, the learner mentioned that her problems with content comprehension were partially due to native speakers' fast speech. EFL learners, particularly those with relatively limited proficiency, appeared to find it challenging to realize adequate content comprehension after watching captioned videos. This learner also pointed out her reliance on captions, stating,

I think after viewing some captioned videos, I became too dependent on the captions. I think I would not watch the videos without captions. (Interviewee 6)

The main point here is the sole dependence on the text. Other learners made similar remarks:

I don't know when I will be confident enough to turn the captions off. (Interviewee 2)

I relied heavily on the captions. Sometimes I replayed or paused the video to see if I could understand the screen text. (Interviewee 4)

Learners also seemed worried about caption quality, reporting that some captions did not appear to convey the speakers' actual language. Such captions could also mislead the learners to some extent:

> I think sometimes the quality of captions was not good. The captions misled me. Sometimes the captions were too big or too small. The words even lagged too far behind compared to what the audio was saying. (Interviewee 3)

Another disadvantage involved learners' habits. Many EFL learners were accustomed to reading printed text. For simple videos, learners reported that the captions were boring and obscured important information:

> I still prefer reading printed text. I am not used to online text. If the video is simple, then captioning can be annoying and seem repetitive. It causes boredom. The captions may block important information on the screen. (Interviewee 5)

Discussion

This chapter highlights the predictive effects of listening and reading comprehension on individuals' learning performance from watching captioned videos. The questionnaire and interview data revealed five key elements: (1) accuracy, (2) comprehension, (3) retention, (4) engagement, and (4) confidence. Accuracy is mainly related to the fact that captions helped learners notice important information, view unfamiliar words or terminology, discern foreign accents, determine the correct spelling of names and terms, and record accurate notes and quotations. Comprehension mostly revolved around captions helping learners visually see key points, connect ideas between the text and visual representations, acquire information in more than one way, learn English as a foreign language, follow the video content, use playback, or pausing for review, and organize information. Retention-related findings indicated that captions helped learners retain information by reading video content, aided in test and exam review, and facilitated information processing. Engagement mainly encompassed the usefulness of captions in helping learners focus on content comprehension or increase their involvement in using videos for language learning. Confidence related mostly to the fact that captions kept learners from becoming bored while watching TV programs. Captions led to learners' greater confidence in listening comprehension, adapting to the rate of speakers' speech, and becoming more attuned to the language input.

Interview data revealed that the accessibility offered by captions transformed EFL students' viewing experiences from only a partial understanding of the plot/story to nearly full or entirely full understanding of the video's plot, characters, dialogue, speech, and accents. Video-watching experiences also became less boring. For example, EFL students perceived watching captioned videos as a valuable activity to enhance their comprehension of the language or culture. Using captioned videos also increased learners' confidence and sense of self-efficacy. Captions made TV program viewing an appealing option in addition to promoting conscious learning and language uptake (Vanderplank, 2016). Many EFL students came to appreciate films in ways they would not have been able to without captions. The nature of viewing changed because learners were drawn to the language shown in captions. Learners' responses indicated that most would choose to learn from captions. In line with previous studies (Pujola, 2002; Winke et al., 2010), learners' need for captions was strong, and the use of captions could trigger their motivation and confidence in language learning. Based on students' self-reports, Graham (2006) found that L2 learners encountered difficulties processing audio input. Learners also perceived captions as a useful technique for dealing with perceptual processing and meaning-making problems. The findings of this chapter thus support the assertion that learners perceive captions to be useful in improving comprehension (Markham, 2001) and helping with speech-stream decoding when learning new words (e.g., Winke et al., 2010).

Captions enabled EFL students to tune in to films' dialogue, especially when plots were complex and speech was fast. They became accustomed to the use of captions and blending listening and reading during the film or program. Captions' functionality was also apparent in shifts in learners' behavior (e.g., less resistance to captions and a greater appreciation for the value of using captions for multiple purposes) (Peters & Webb, 2018). Objectives for captions included comprehending a complex plot, becoming accustomed to dialects and accents, and understanding the cultural context for the videos. Captions thus became more than a cultural artifact in a foreign language; they also represented a stimulus for language acquisition.

According to interview data, some EFL learners perceived printed materials as a more accessible medium and TV programs and films as more complicated, with full, confident comprehension of TV programs a seemingly unreachable goal. EFL learners' self-efficacy in watching

TV programs may have been somewhat lower than when reading printed text. Opportunities to use audiovisual media as resources for EFL learning were constrained. Many EFL students perceived audiovisual media as lacking to the extent that they could not fully engage with it. Based on learners' comments, captions did not seem to help these students understand complex, ambiguous, or new material; they still needed to invest great effort in processing language input. The quality of captions was also problematic. Some students decided that some captions were above their proficiency level or of poor quality. Some students' learning behavior was also a concern: they became dependent on captions to the point that they were reluctant to turn them off. In addition, some learners relied heavily on reading captions. Some noted that when they focused on the captions, they could not focus on the sound or music in the video. Even with captions, it was still difficult for some learners to understand a particular language. However, the negative comments included in this chapter do not suggest that captioned videos are futile for language learning. Instead, learners need more graded practice when viewing captioned videos. More specifically, L2 learners should not be deprived of the massive quantities of authentic language otherwise unattainable in language classrooms. Text-supported viewing may decrease learners' stress levels when facing ungraded and authentic language, thus facilitating language acquisition and retention. Learners may also need to view carefully selected captioned programs routinely. Through well-designed captioned programs or videos, learners may develop conscious, critical faculties, the ability to draw language (and linguistic features) from programs, and the capacity to incorporate newly learned language into their own repertoire.

Concluding Remarks

Numerous studies had been conducted to investigate the effects of captions on the cognitive processing of language learners. Most studies focused on the effects of captions on learners' language learning enhancement. Since information and communication technology has been growing at a breakneck pace, such development provides learners with limitless interactive materials. Directing learners to achieve the utmost benefit from the materials is essential for language teacher educators to consider. If learners are unable to receive guidance in what materials to use and how to use them, they may become confused. Without instruction, learners may become demotivated from learning. Thus, enabling learners to use authentic materials as effectively as possible is necessary. In this regard, captions are authentic language learning materials that may motivate language learners. This chapter presented some student observations that confirmed the benefits of captions. Captions can aid learners' comprehension, and as a result, learners become motivated for language learning. The visual aids in captioned videos can help learners comprehend aural input. Hence, actively engaging learners in the language learning process is helpful. Learners' memory works better when both their auditory and visual registers are stimulated. Through using captions as a means of interaction and modifying input, learners' affective filter can be lowered. Captions can consolidate what they have learned.

When applying captions to future classroom instruction, certain questions need to be considered. First, captions can be a source for learning words and grammar rules. However, whether captions are suitable for all learners from beginner to advanced proficiency levels needs to be taken into account. Teng (2019a) documented learners' language proficiency level as the main factor that affected the learning outcome from captioned videos. We may need to consider how to maximize the effectiveness of captioned videos or programs for learners of different proficiency levels. Second, motivation is one of the key components that affect language learning (Man, Bui, & Teng, 2018). Becoming over-reliant on printed materials may make learning linguistic, structural rules monotonous for learners. We need to consider how to motivate learners' language learning performance through the use of captions. Third, although captions have been used a lot for enhancing vocabulary, considering word exposure frequency in captioned videos is an emerging topic in future research (Teng, 2019b). Finally, advance organizer activities prior to video viewing is another possible option to contemplate (Teng, 2019c).

References

Baddeley, A. D. (1992). Working memory. *Science*, 255(1), 556–559.
Graham, S. (2006). Listening comprehension: The learners' perspective. *System*, 34(2), 165–182.
Man, L., Bui, G., & Teng, F. (2018). From second language to third language learning: Exploring a dual-motivation system among multilinguals. *Australian Review of Applied Linguistics*, 41 (1), 63–91.
Markham, P. (2001). The influence of culture-specific background knowledge and captions on second language comprehension. *Journal of Educational Technology Systems*, 29(4), 331–343.

Montero Perez, M., Peters, E., Clarebout, G., & Desmet, P. (2014). Effects of captioning on video comprehension and incidental vocabulary learning. *Language Learning & Technology, 18*(1), 118–141.

Park, M. (2004). *The effects of partial captions on Korean EFL learners' listening comprehension.* Unpublished doctoral dissertation, University of Texas at Austin.

Peters, E., & Webb, S. (2018). Incidental vocabulary acquisition through viewing L2 television and factors that affect learning. *Studies in Second Language Acquisition, 40*(3), 551–577.

Plass, J. L., & Jones, L. C. (2005). Multimedia learning in second language acquisition. In R. E. Mayer (Ed.), *The Cambridge handbook of multimedia learning* (pp. 467–488). New York, NY, US: Cambridge University Press.

Pujola, J.-T. (2002). CALLing for help: Researching language learning strategies using help facilities in a web-based multimedia program. *ReCALL, 14*(2), 235–262.

Sweller, J. (2005). The redundancy principle in multimedia learning. In R. Mayer (Ed.), *The Cambridge handbook of multimedia learning* (pp. 159–168). New York: Cambridge University Press.

Teng, F. (2019a). *Maximizing the potential of captions for primary school ESL students' comprehension of English-language videos. Computer Assisted Language Learning, 32*(7), 665–691. Doi: 10.1080/09588221.2018.1532912.

Teng, F. (2019b). Incidental vocabulary learning for primary school students: The effects of L2 caption type and word exposure frequency. *The Australian Educational Researcher, 46*(1), 113–136.

Teng, F. (2019c). *The effects of video caption types and advance organizers on incidental L2 collocation learning. Computers & Education, 142,* 103655. Doi: 10.1016/j.compedu.2019.103655.

Vanderplank, R. (1988). The value of teletext sub-titles in language learning. *English Language Teaching Journal, 42*(4), 272–281.

Vanderplank, R. (2016). *Captioned media in foreign language learning and teaching: Subtitles for the deaf and hard-of-hearing as tools for language learning.* Oxford: Palgrave Macmillan.

Wickens, C. D. (2007). Attention to the second language. *IRAL, 45*(3), 177–191.

Winke, P., Gass, S., & Sydorenko, T. (2010). The effects of captioning videos used for foreign language listening activities. *Language Learning & Technology, 14*(1), 65–86.

4 Vocabulary Learning From Captioned Videos for EFL Learners

Captions are beneficial for vocabulary building. During my experiences of teaching EFL to Chinese students, I used episodes of well-known situation comedies, e.g., *Friends*, to teach my students. The main reasons for choosing those videos were to arouse my students' interest, attract their attention, and help them gain more cultural knowledge. I felt that my students were always timid when speaking in English in public. In addition, they would frequently attempt to memorize some words without referring to the context. I deliberately chose captioned videos for my students and felt that they could learn more words and expressions and some cultural knowledge from the videos. Most importantly, they could have certain topics to practice and develop their speaking.

I proposed the use of captioned videos for several reasons. The first reason was that learners could most effectively understand linguistic and content information from captioned videos. The second reason was that EFL learners, unlike native speakers, did not have sufficient exposure to English input. Exposure to authentic printed texts might not be adequate for enhancing learners' language development. The texts accompanied by captions become a specific type of technique for learners' comprehension and vocabulary learning. The third reason was that captions fostered learners' abilities in becoming accustomed to speakers' rapid delivery speed. Adapting to the sounds of the second language is much like bottom-up (progressive) training in listening skills. In particular, captioning accommodates segmenting words and chunks of languages while listening to the stream of speech. Finally, captioning helps learners develop a range of strategies to compensate for comprehension difficulties. Methods included both bottom-up and top-down cognitive strategies. For example, getting the gist of keywords from captions, using auditory and visual cues to infer the meaning of unknown words, predicting forthcoming content, and understanding contextual clues for sentence meaning. The use of captioning then allowed me—as the teacher—to tap into a wide range of genres that captivated my students.

Captioned Videos and Vocabulary Learning

A critical area of interest is examining evidence that captioned viewing may lead to enhancement in vocabulary learning. Developing vocabulary learning from captioned videos is difficult, especially in foreign language learning contexts. Vocabulary learning becomes more challenging due to the dynamic and fast-paced nature of TV and films. So far, studies have provided some evidence for the support of captioned viewing for vocabulary learning. The focus on captioned viewing helps learners comprehend the content and build a form-meaning link for some new words. Indeed, captioned viewing can help learners understand bottom-up phonological skills. Many factors, including speech stream chunking, word recognition, a lack of vocabulary knowledge, and a lack of word recognition skills, influence the outcome of vocabulary learning from captioned viewing.

Existing studies have explored the effectiveness of captions in enhancing vocabulary. For example, Montero Perez, Peters, Clarebout, and Desmet (2014) investigated the effects of types of captioning on incidental learning of unknown words by university students across four experimental groups. The first group watched videos without captions ($n = 32$); the second watched videos with captioned keywords ($n = 34$); the third watched fully captioned videos ($n = 30$); and the fourth watched fully captioned videos with highlighted keywords ($n = 37$). Results indicated that captioning did not affect meaning recall (i.e., ability to supply the meaning of a target word), but greatly enhanced form recognition (i.e., ability to identify the correct target word). Although captions appeared to have the potential to help learners build form-meaning connections in their mental lexicon, captions were more helpful for recognizing the meaning of new words (Neuman & Koskinen, 1992). In contrast to Winke, Gass, and Sydorenko's (2010) findings that revealed a beneficial effect of captioning on meaning recall, recalling target word meanings with the help of captioning appeared to remain challenging for some students. As acknowledged by Montero Perez et al. (2014), the reasons included: (a) captioning provided little information regarding the meaning of difficult words, rendering meaning construction based on learners' inferred process unreliable; (b) learners were not given sufficient time to infer word meaning from context while watching the videos; (c) inferring word meaning was a challenging and unsuccessful process, and (d) the meaning recall test administered to the learners after viewing the video one time was too demanding.

Similarly, Peters, Heynen, and Puimège (2016) conducted two exploratory studies investigating the effect of the first language (L1) subtitles and captions on various aspects of word knowledge (i.e., form recognition and meaning recall). Findings showed a positive effect of captions on the word form learning, but not on the learning of meaning for the Belgian English learners. Two factors contributed to these results: learners' vocabulary size and the frequency with which the target words occurred. Montero Perez, Peters, and Desmet (2018) recently focused on measuring the effects of L2 captioning types (i.e., no captioning, keyword captioning, full-captioning, and glossed keyword captioning) and test announcement (i.e., informing vs. not informing students that a vocabulary test would be administered after viewing the video) on incidental vocabulary learning. A total of 227 Dutch-speaking university students participated in the study. Findings revealed that students exposed to glossed keyword captioning scored highest on form recognition and meaning recall. However, the test announcement did not affect vocabulary learning results. Factors influencing test results included learners' vocabulary size and their look-up behavior in the glossed keyword condition.

Three general conclusions can be drawn from these studies. Although partial learning gains were demonstrated, the captions potentially helped learners construct an initial form-meaning map in their mental lexicon. This result suggests that captions helped learners recognize the form and meaning of target words. Second, although captioning was a powerful tool in assisting learners in recognizing word form and meaning, learners still encountered significant challenges in recalling word meaning. The success rate of captioning appeared to be dependent on the test modality, namely, the aspect of word knowledge being tested. Noticing form is the first step in the vocabulary-learning process (Hulstijn, 2001) but is neither linear nor guaranteed to lead to a meaning recall. As proposed by the noticing hypothesis, the input does not become intake for language learning unless it is noticed (i.e., consciously registered) (Schmidt, 1990, 2001). Third, captions facilitated learners' attentional resources in comprehending the novel words that appeared in a video. The comprehension was a conscious selection process based on noting and gathering information, which might have helped learners reflect on and notice disparities while comparing their L2 knowledge with captioned video input.

These studies point to the need to develop vocabulary knowledge for students in a second or foreign language learning context. As argued by Teng (2020), the development of vocabulary knowledge is dependent on the strategies for captioned viewing. Through engaging students with advanced organizer strategies, some degree of form-meaning mapping is taking place. The form-meaning link facilitates students' development of the phonological characteristics of sounds and words as they are uttered in connected speech. While processing visual and verbal information, the different channels did not inhibit but enhanced the students' efficient use of processing strategies for audiovisual input. Although existing studies generally agree upon the benefits of captions in the context of language learning, further investigation is required to determine the potential of captions on facilitating incidental vocabulary learning.

A Selection of Studies on Enhancing Vocabulary Learning From Captioned Viewing

Many recent studies that address the effects of captioned videos on vocabulary learning have been published. These studies certainly expand the field further. This section describes some recent studies on using captions for examining possible improvements in vocabulary learning.

Teng, F. (2019a) Incidental Vocabulary Learning for Primary School Students: The Effects of L2 Caption Type and Word Exposure Frequency. The Australian Educational Researcher

Captioned videos may offer a new perspective on exploring incidental vocabulary learning. However, I claimed that if learners were not allowed to return to a previous word or sentence while watching videos, vocabulary learning through audiovisual input could be limited due to rapid online processing demands and the difficulties in guessing unknown words (see details on Teng, 2019a). Based on this research gap, I suggested a need to investigate the interplay between types of captions and word exposure frequency for incidental vocabulary learning. Previous studies have only analyzed these two options separately. Research combining the use of captions and word-exposure frequency for students' vocabulary learning remains underexplored. This deserves more attention for primary school ESL learners who often have limited English proficiency and tend to stay away from printed reading material because of their difficulties with processing

Vocabulary Learning From Captioned Vidoes 57

English syntax, vocabulary, phonological representations, figurative language, and word retention). Thus, Teng's (2019a) focus was to combine captioned videos and word exposure frequency, providing theoretical and practical possibilities to enhance incidental vocabulary learning in primary school students. The focus was on primary school ESL learners' incidental learning of new lexical items while watching videos. Two variables were considered, both alone and in combination: the frequency of exposure to target words (one occurrence and three occurrences) and the type of captioning (full captioning, keyword captioning, and no captions).

Teng set out three research questions:

1. To what extent does incidental learning of new words differ between three captioning types—full captioning, keyword captions, and no captions—when the three conditions include the same number of encounters with target words?
2. To what extent does the incidental learning of new words differ between the two conditions involving different word occurrence frequencies (i.e., one and three) for each captioning type?
3. To what extent does incidental learning of new words differ between specific combinations of word exposure frequency and captioning conditions?

Research Design

Teng adopted a 2 × 3 between-subjects design. The first independent variable was the frequency of target word exposure (one occurrence and three occurrences). The second independent variable was the type of captioning: full captions, keyword captions, and no captions, as recommended by Montero Perez, Peters, and Desmet (2013). The combination of these independent variables resulted in six experimental groups. Details on the combinations of various types of captioning and word encounter frequencies among the six groups are shown in Table 4.1. Participants included 257 students from six primary schools. The number of participants in each group is presented in Table 4.1.

Video Selection

A clip from a series of English video stories for young learners was selected for this study. The video *Polar Exploration* was chosen, which shows how scientists use robots to explore underwater

58 *Vocabulary Learning From Captioned Vidoes*

Table 4.1 Combination of the Various Types of Captioning and Word Encounter Frequency in the Six Groups

Captioning Types	Word Encounter Frequency: 3 Times	Word Encounter Frequency: 1 Time
Full captioning	Group 1: Full captioning + 3-times word occurrence ($n = 46$)	Group 2: Full captioning + 1-time word occurrence ($n = 42$)
Keyword captioning	Group 3: Keyword captioning + 3-times word occurrence ($n = 43$)	Group 4: Keyword captioning + 1-time word occurrence ($n = 43$)
No captioning	Group 5: No captioning + 3-times word occurrence ($n = 42$)	Group 6: No captioning + 1-time word occurrence ($n = 41$)

mountain ranges in the Arctic Ocean. A short video with a certain number of target words occurring three times was unavailable. Scripts were discussed and edited to allow for target words occurring three times in appropriate contexts.

Captions

Captions were added through MAGpie. Full captions represented verbatim transcription of dialogue, and keyword captions represented a single word (e.g., decorate) or a maximum of three consecutive words (e.g., strong and courageous). Keywords were defined as those words in a sentence that was essential for the learners to construct meaning.

Target Words and Vocabulary Test

Potential target words were selected from the video clip. Teachers selected 15 items from the scripts. This test consisted of three parts. The first part measured receptive form recognition in which the learners were required to choose "yes" if the target word appeared in the clip or "no" if it did not. If learners selected "yes," the computer automatically proceeded to the next part, which measured meaning recall. If learners selected "no," the computer instead moved to the next word. The meaning recall test was a productive test in which learners were required to provide the L1 translation of a given target item. Following this step, learners were oriented to a multiple-choice word meaning recognition test. They were required to select the correct response from four Chinese translations (e.g., luxurious: A. 漂亮的 B.可愛的 C. 奢侈的 or D. 真實的). All test parts were scored binomially, awarding one point for a correct answer and zero for an incorrect answer.

Results

Within the 'one-word occurrence' condition, full captioning appeared to lead to a better outcome than the keyword captioning and no captions. Within the 'three-word occurrences' condition, full captioning also led to better performance than keyword captioning and no captions. Within each captioning condition, three-times word occurrences also yielded better performance than a single occurrence. Overall, the group exposed to full captioning with target words occurring thrice demonstrated the best performance among the groups. The results showed a significant main effect of type of captioning on the three test parts [Wilk's lambda F(3, 254) = 19.20, $p < .05$, $\eta^2 = .08$]. The analysis also revealed a significant main effect of word exposure frequency on the three test parts [Wilk's lambda F(3, 254) = 18.20, $p < .05$, $\eta^2 = .07$]. A significant interaction effect was not detected between the type of captioning and word exposure frequency [Wilk's lambda F(3, 254) = 18.26, $p > .05$]. These patterns suggest that type of captioning and word exposure frequency each exerted a pronounced effect on the learning of new words. Overall, the combination of three encounters and the full captioning condition yielded the best results, which were significantly better than any of the other five combinations. This finding remained consistent across all dimensions of the vocabulary test.

The Effectiveness of Captioning on Vocabulary Learning

Based on Teng's findings, the benefits from using fully captioned videos in incidental vocabulary learning could be explained through Baddeley's (1986) working memory model, wherein the use of two separate perceptual domains (i.e., a visual and verbal task) do not interfere with each other. The coordination of verbal associations and visual imagery is governed by the central executive—a supervisory system that controls the flow of information—and the episodic buffer, a limited capacity system that provides temporary storage of information (Baddeley, 2000). In other words, while learners receive imagery information, they may be able to derive verbal information from the auditory channel, supporting a dual-modal presentation technique (Xu, Fang, Brzezinski, & Chan, 2008). These results can also be explained through Paivio's (1986) dual coding theory. According to Paivio, perceptual associations with image coding and semantic associations with verbal coding reinforces connections between the dual-modal representations. In other words, coding a stimulus (in this case, vocabulary) in two distinct ways promotes more effective recall than if the stimulus were coded through either representation alone.

The Effectiveness of Word Encounter Frequency on Vocabulary Learning

Participants demonstrated greater gains in learning new words when target words were encountered more often. This observation confirmed previous studies (e.g., Peters et al., 2016; Teng, 2018a), wherein repeated encounters with unknown words increased the likelihood of noticing these items. Repeated encounters with target words may help learners attend to and notice linguistic features of input (Schmidt, 2001). Incidental vocabulary learning is largely a side effect of linguistic processing, in which attention must be focused. Word encounter frequency appeared to help learners focus on word form (i.e., pronunciation and spelling) along with the available cues in audiovisual input that can lead to meaning identification, encouraging more effective incidental vocabulary learning. Additionally, the frequency effect resulted in substantial improvements in incidental vocabulary learning irrespective of the captioning type, contributing to knowledge in this line of research.

The combination of full captioning and three encounters of a word greatly enhanced incidental word learning. Students learned a notable degree of vocabulary knowledge, especially in recognizing form-meaning links. Students' performance in Teng's study was more encouraging than results from a recent study (Montero Perez et al., 2018). The effect of word encounter frequency on the full captioning condition appeared to improve incidental vocabulary learning further. Given these positive results, the combination of full captioning and three encounters could be argued to have reduced learners' decoding load and provided them more time to allocate attention toward interpretation (e.g., Markham, Peter, & McCarthy, 2001; Pulido, 2007; Rodgers & Webb, 2017) or reduced demand for cognitive workload required for information comprehension (Peters et al., 2016), and thus establish a form-meaning link (Winke et al., 2010).

Main Implication of the Study

The disappointing results of meaning recall provided insights into reframing Schmidt's (1990, 2001) noticing hypothesis. Captioned videos offered comprehensible input (Krashen, 1985). However, Teng (2019a) argued that tracking genuine intake from captioned input to recalling word meaning in a decontextualized scenario still presented a marked challenge for primary school ESL learners. Simply having access to comprehensible input does not mean that extraction and recall of word meaning will occur seamlessly (Qin & Teng, 2017; Teng, 2018b). The actions of noticing and attending are fleeting, situated at the bottom of the affective pyramid in cognitive and affective taxonomy, lower than "responding" and "valuing" and very far from internalizing (Vanderplank, 2016, p. 243). Hence, learners need time to develop their own conscious and critical faculties to draw word meaning from captioned videos and build it into their own competencies.

Teng (2019b) Maximizing the Potential of Captions for Primary School ESL Students' Comprehension of English-language Videos. Computer Assisted Language Learning.

New evidence has supported the use of captions in enhancing learners' comprehension (e.g., Rodgers & Webb, 2017). Captioned videos appear to be an effective means of instruction for helping learners grasp the gist of visual cues. In particular, visual associations created in memory along with the mnemonic power of imagery may increase the comprehensibility of video input by helping students associate words with actual objects and encourage them to learn imaging techniques. These developments could ultimately lead to better comprehension in ESL learning. However, research on using captions for primary school students' comprehension remains under-explored.

The reciprocal relationship between captioned videos and English comprehension could increase understanding of word-based knowledge and background knowledge. These developments are necessary to overcome obstacles in school children's reading comprehension, such as a failure to figure out the connection between written and spoken words, an inability to decode and recognize words from text reading, and a lack of motivation to read (National Research Council, 1998). However, comprehension by ESL learners with limited English proficiency may be hindered by difficulties involving English syntax, vocabulary, phonological representations, and text structures.

Teng's (2019b) study sought to address this gap by examining the effects of three captioning types—full captioning, keyword captioning, and no captioning—on video content comprehension. To enhance knowledge in this area, two variables (i.e., learners' language proficiency and the number of times the video is viewed) were also examined. Despite previous research indicating the significant influence these variables (full caption vs. keyword captioning, English proficiency level, and word exposure frequency) have on learning effects, his study was the first one that thoroughly and simultaneously examined their effect on enhancing primary school ESL learners' English comprehension. He set out four research questions:

1. Are any of the treatments (i.e., full-captioning videos, keyword-captioning videos, and videos without captions) superior to the others in terms of video content comprehension for ESL primary school students with different proficiency levels?
2. To what extent do learners with higher and lower English proficiency differ under each of the three captioning conditions?
3. Are any of the treatments (i.e., full-captioning videos, keyword-captioning videos, and videos without captions) superior to the others in terms of video content comprehension when videos are watched once or twice?
4. Does repeated watching of captioned videos lead to better performance in video content comprehension under any of the three captioning conditions?

Research Design

Data were subjected to a 2 × 2 × 3 analysis of variance (ANOVA) using three treatments (i.e., full-captioning videos, keyword-captioning videos, and videos without captions), two levels of English proficiency (low vs. high), and two videos (watched once vs. twice). Each group was split into two subgroups (i.e., low vs. high proficiency) according to an internal standardized English test. Dependent variables for measuring participants' possible enhancement in language comprehension included a written recall protocol instrument and an open-ended test. The Newman–Keuls method, a stepwise multiple comparisons procedure, was employed to identify whether group differences were statistically significant at the 0.05 level. In total, 182 sixth-grade students from three primary schools were recruited for this study (Table 4.2).

Table 4.2 Participants' Characteristics and Reading Performance by Group

	Group 1 (School A, Fully Captioned Group)	Group 2 (School B, Keyword-Captioned Group)	Group 3 (School C, no Captions)
Gender			
Female	32	32	33
Male	30	31	24
Language proficiency			
Low achievers	30	31	30
High achievers	32	32	27
Total number	62	63	57

Materials

Two different English-language videos were selected for the three experimental groups. Video 1 (10 m 28 s) was a short video, *Snowy Day*. Video 2 (10 m 20 s) was a short video, *To Catch a Thief*.

Measures

Two comprehension tests were developed for each video: a written recall protocol instrument and a multiple-choice test. The first dependent measure determined students' global comprehension. Participants were required to write a summary of the video content in English. This test was intended to measure participants' ability to recall their comprehension of the text materials without the constraints of responding to questions posed by others. A maximum of 20 points were awarded to learners who could produce a reasonable number of idea units and elaborations without distortions and errors.

In the second dependent measure, learners were asked to choose the best alternatives from four options for each question. The learners completed 20 multiple-choice items immediately after watching a video. All questions focused on the details of the video content. The items were developed with a focus on keywords but could not be answered directly without understanding the content; this format ensured that the questions addressed important information and discard irrelevant information. Also, group differences could not be plausibly compared without focusing on the captioned keywords. One example of this test is as follows:

Table 4.3 2 × 2 × 3 Analysis of Variance on the Written Recall Protocol Instrument Scores

Source	df	Sum of Square	Mean Square	F	p
Treatment	2	261.562	87.187	11.038	.000**
Performance	1	136.782	136.782	11.221	.001**
Video	1	39.512	39.512	11.352	.000**
Treatment × Performance	2	89.862	29.954	9.113	.005**
Treatment × Video	2	83.678	27.892	9.344	.004**
Performance × Video	1	88.336	88.336	7.321	.044*
Treatment × Performance × Video	2	85.562	28.52	7.421	.039*
Error	179	3044.52			
Total	182	3829.814			

Notes
*$p < .05$.
**$p < .01$.

1   Why was Kate unwilling to join the party?

   A   She needs a break
   B   She is driving a car
   C   She needs to work on her application for school
   D   She is making a call

One point was allotted to each correct answer with a possible total score of 20.

Results

The results of the 2 × 2 × 3 ANOVA are presented in Table 4.3.

The Newman–Keuls test showed that the treatment with fully captioned videos resulted in significantly higher scores than the treatment with keyword-captioned videos ($p < .05$); and the treatment with keyword-captioned videos produced significantly higher scores than the treatment without captions ($p < .05$). This outcome was consistent across high and low proficiency learners, suggesting that fully captioned videos constituted the most effective means of increasing learners' global comprehension, regardless of proficiency level. The Newman–Keuls test also showed that learners with higher English language proficiency scored significantly higher than those with lower English language proficiency ($p < .05$). This result was consistent across the three groups, indicating that high proficiency learners outperformed low proficiency learners in global comprehension irrespective of the captioning condition. Overall, learners with high English proficiency in the fully captioned group achieved the best global comprehension.

The Newman–Keuls test results also revealed that watching video 2 for the second time yielded better performance than watching video 1 once ($p < .05$). This result was consistent across the three captioning groups, implying that repeated viewing of captioned videos led to better global comprehension in each of the three captioning conditions. Overall, learners who watched the video twice in the fully captioned condition achieved the best results on the written assessment.

Key Findings for Research Questions

The first question explored the different effects of the three treatments (full-captioning videos, keyword-captioning videos, and videos without captions) on video comprehension for ESL primary school students with different proficiency levels. Results showed that fully captioned videos were more effective for high proficiency learners' video comprehension, including global and detailed comprehension. Although fully captioned videos were also effective for low-proficiency learners' global comprehension, no significant difference appeared between full-captioning videos and keyword-captioning videos for learners with low proficiency.

The second question explored comprehension differences between learners with higher and lower English proficiency under each of the three captioning conditions. Results indicated that students with higher proficiency outperformed those with lower proficiency in each condition.

The third question explored the differences in comprehension between the three captioning types when a video was watched either once or twice. Results implied that when the video was watched twice, the effectiveness of the fully captioned condition was outstanding for global and detailed comprehension. However, when the video was watched only once, the effectiveness of the fully captioned condition on global comprehension was detected, whereas it was negligible on detailed comprehension.

The fourth question explored whether repeated watching of captioned videos led to better performance in video comprehension for each of the three captioning conditions. Results demonstrated the effectiveness of watching the video twice rather than once for each captioning condition.

Discussion and Theoretical Implication

Given the positive results obtained across two differently captioned groups for the written recall protocol instrument, full captions may have reduced learners' decoding load and allowed them to devote attention to meaning interpretation, as revealed in other empirical studies (e.g., Montero Perez et al., 2018; Pulido, 2007; Rodgers & Webb, 2017). In particular, the use of full captioning appeared to promote ESL primary school learners' engagement in comprehending important elements in the story and thus helped them recall the video content more thoroughly. However, the effectiveness of fully captioned videos on English comprehension, including global comprehension and detailed comprehension, was more significant for learners with high proficiency and those who watched the videos twice. For learners with low proficiency and those who watched the videos only once, the effectiveness of fully captioned videos on detailed comprehension was not significant. This finding indicates that primary school ESL learners, who may have trouble understanding a rapid, authentic native speaker in a video until they have gained considerable exposure to it (Linebarger, 2001; Markham et al., 2001), differed in their performance in global comprehension and detailed comprehension. Fully captioned videos may help primary school ESL learners improve global comprehension, which is in line with Montero Perez et al.'s (2013) study that found that full captioning led to greater gains in global comprehension (i.e., writing the summary of a video story when measured immediately after viewing a video) compared to keyword captioning and no captioning.

One theoretical explanation of the results indicates learners' proficiency levels played a key role in dictating whether they could be engaged with captioned videos. As suggested by Yeldham (2018), more proficient learners may be more likely to engage with the multiple cues embedded in captions and visuals. Differences in comprehension between high-proficiency and low-proficiency learners may enrich Mayer's (2009) cognitive load theory. First, L2 learners seem to have constraints on their working memory when processing the information, as noted by Baddeley (2000). Such limitations on working memory may hinder learners' ability to simultaneously handle the verbal and imagery systems proposed in Paivio's (1986) dual-coding theory. Second, L2 learners with low proficiency may have limited working memory when processing aural and visual information. However, Vanderplank (2016) contended that watching captioned videos did not overwhelm the viewer with bimodal input but instead offered multiple representations of the same input to help learners better comprehend video information. Hence, learners with low proficiency levels may become overloaded and unable to process the multiple representations of information required per the multimedia principle (Fletcher & Tobias, 2005). This finding is inconsistent with the parallel processing model (Taylor, 2005), wherein learners can use various cognitive channels to process multiple sources of information. This pattern may apply to learners with high proficiency, as this model characterizes learners as being able to comprehend information automatically without devoting much working memory to handling multiple cues. Third, learners who watched the video for a second time may have developed strategies to compensate for difficulties comprehending the video information. This development likely involved strategies of planning, monitoring, and evaluating the comprehension process; predicting forthcoming information; and discerning unknown meaning (Teng, 2018c; Teng & Huang, 2019). Finally, detailed comprehension has been shown to be challenging for L2 learners, as they may need to narrow their cognitive focus to evaluate detailed information. In practice, L2 learners in such a position may favor overall comprehension over attending to or recalling detailed information. In a setting where video images and captioned information are presented together, learners would be expected to exploit the aural conduit. However, the benefits of resorting to captions for detailed comprehension, a skill requiring a complex cognitive process, and exerted effort for primary school ESL learners, may warrant further study.

Teng (2019c) The Effects of Video Caption Types and Advance Organizers on Incidental L2 Collocation Learning. Computers & Education.

Teng's (2019c) study focused on incidental learning of collocations from captioned videos. Inclusion of collocations—a type of multi-word unit—has been suggested as a prerequisite for achieving advanced levels of language proficiency and fluency in the second language (L2) learning (Schmitt, 2010). Despite efforts to explore best practices in the teaching and learning of individual words, research on L2 vocabulary development has only recently started to examine learning performance in relation to multi-word units, including collocations (Webb & Nation, 2017). L2 learners' multiple-word units acquisition has been found to lag behind single-word acquisition (e.g., Pellicer-Sánchez, 2017); even when learners produce multi-word units, they may demonstrate inappropriate usage (e.g., Nesselhauf, 2005). Moreover, L2 learners may not have sufficient intuition to determine the frequency of collocations and then process or learn them (Siyanova-Chanturia & Spina, 2015). Schmitt (2010) contended that compared to the acquisition of single words, collocations and other multi-word units pose unique challenges for L2 learners.

Hence, identifying effective ways to maximize the incidental learning of collocations is essential. This approach to learning vocabulary operates by focusing the learners' attention on discerning the meanings of messages without deliberately committing the items to memory (Hulstijn, 2013). Incidental learning of collocations through audiovisual inputs may be challenging because of rapid online processing demands while inferring meanings of collocations from literal concepts. To address the limited effects of captioned videos, and advance-organizer strategy (AOS) has been suggested as an approach for strengthening L2 learners' capacity to associate prior knowledge with audiovisual input in a multimedia environment for a better interpretation and comprehension of the material (Li, 2014). Incidental learning of collocations through the interplay of captions and an AOS has not yet been explored.

Therefore, Teng examined the incidental learning of collocations through two independent variables: either the presence or absence of an AOS, and the type of captioning in videos (i.e., full captioning, keyword captioning, or no captions). Teng's study was novel in its collective evaluation of an AOS and captions. Findings provide insights for pedagogical decisions and enable L2 teachers to identify more effective methods for incidental learning of collocations in a multimedia classroom setting. Teng set out three research questions:

1 What is the main effect of an AOS on L2 young learners' incidental learning of collocations?
2 What is the main effect of captioned videos on L2 young learners' incidental learning of collocations?
3 What is the interaction effect of captioned videos and an AOS strategy on L2 young learners' incidental learning of collocations?

Research Design

The present study adopted a 2 × 3 between-subjects design. The two independent variables were captioning types, i.e., full captioning, keyword captioning, and videos without captions (Montero Perez et al., 2013), and an AOS (Li, 2014). The AOS refers to a teaching strategy that helps L2 learners integrate prior knowledge and organize their thoughts and ideas for improved input comprehension by exercising given 'known' information in videos (Teng, 2020). The two independent variables resulted in six experimental groups. Group 1 viewed full-captioning videos and completed advance-organizer exercises (FC + AO, $n = 59$). Group 2 viewed full-captioning videos without advance-organizer exercises (FC, $n = 67$). Group 3 viewed keyword-captioning videos and completed advance-organizer exercises (KC + AO, $n = 54$). Group 4 viewed keyword-captioning videos without advance-organizer exercises (KC, $n = 61$). Group 5 viewed videos without captions and completed advance-organizer exercises (NC + AO, $n = 58$). Finally, Group 6 viewed videos without captions and did not participate in advance-organizer exercises (NC, $n = 62$). The internal test was administered to 100 sixth-grade students in each school prior to the study. From among the students in each group, 61, 57, 58, 68, 61, and 62 learners earned 80–85 points out of 100 and were selected as participants. ANOVA comparing the six groups' performances on this test did not reveal a significant difference in scores. The effects of captioned videos and advance organizers on incidental learning of collocations were measured using a two-way multivariate ANOVA.

Videos

Four authentic episodes were selected from a series of YouTube storytelling videos for children. Each episode was approximately 10 minutes long, which allowed several collocations to be inserted.

Measures

A total of 16 verb-noun collocations that were considered challenging for L2 learners were selected. In the first section, which measured productive knowledge of form, learners were required to write collocates based on a given word. Learners were also instructed to write the correct verb that had been encountered in the stories for the given noun. In the following example, participants were asked to supply the missing target collocate (exaggerate) next to the word "facts":

_____ facts

The second part was a multiple-choice test to measure receptive knowledge of form. Each item included five options: the correct collocate, three plausible distracters, and one "I don't know" option to reduce random guessing. For example,

    _____ facts

A determine
B exaggerate
C imagine
D decorate E. I don't know

The third part measured productive knowledge of the meaning and was presented in a translation format; learners used L1 meanings to write L2 collocations. This test was intended to identify whether learners had incidentally learned the form and meaning of the collocations. For instance, learners were asked to write the English collocation (exaggerate facts) next to its L1 translation:

    夸大事實 _____

The fourth part measured receptive knowledge of meaning in a receptive translation format. This test included L2 collocations as cues, and learners were instructed to write down the L1 meanings. In the following example, learners were asked to write the L1 meaning for the collocation "exaggerate facts":

    exaggerate facts _____

Results

Under each captioning condition, the use of the AOS yielded higher scores than the absence of the advance-organizer technique. In addition, under each advance-organizer condition, full captioning led to higher scores, followed by keyword captioning and no captions. Among the six groups, the FC + AO group achieved the best results on the four test parts (productive form: 5.36; receptive form: 9.76; productive meaning: 7.12; receptive meaning: 12.37).

Table 4.4 presents the multivariate test results. The Wilks' lambda results revealed differences between the group means on dependent variables. Based on significance values of the F-ratios, findings

Table 4.4 Multivariate Test Results

Multivariate Test[a]

Effect		Value	F	Hypothesis df	Error df	P	Partial Eta Squared
Intercept	Wilks' lambda	0.010	5611.157[b]	4.000	231.000	0.000	0.990
Advance organizers	Wilks' lambda	0.258	165.814[b]	4.000	231.000	0.000	0.742
Captioned videos	Wilks' lambda	0.116	111.905[b]	8.000	462.000	0.000	0.660
Advance organizers * captioned videos	Wilks' lambda	0.053	82.026[b]	8.000	462.000	0.029	0.622

Notes
[a]Design: Intercept + advance organizers + captioned videos + advance organizers * captioned videos.
[b]Exact statistic.

indicated a statistically significant effect of the advance-organizer intervention on learners' incidental learning of collocations [F(4, 231) = 165.814, $p < .001$; Wilks' $\Lambda = .258$, partial $\eta^2 = .742$]. A statistically significant effect also appeared for captioned videos on incidental learning of collocations [F(8, 462) = 111.905, $p < .001$; Wilks' $\Lambda = .116$, partial $\eta^2 = .660$]. A statistically significant interaction effect of advance organizers and types of captioned videos on the combined dependent variables [F(8, 462) = 82.026, $p < .05$; Wilks' $\Lambda = .053$, partial $\eta^2 = .062$] was found.

Overall, these patterns suggest that both captioning type and AOS had a pronounced effect on the incidental learning of collocations. In particular, the combination of using AOS in the full captioning condition yielded significantly better results than any of the other five combinations. This was consistent for learning all four dimensions of collocation knowledge.

Discussion and Implications

Findings highlight the effect of an AOS on incidental learning of collocations for L2 learners. These results correspond with those from research on the facilitative role of an advance organizer in enhancing L2 learning (Chung & Huang, 1998; Herron, 1994; Li, 2014). In a recent study conducted by Teng (2020), wherein a total of 240 Chinese students were randomly and equally assigned to eight conditions. The eight conditions were formed through two independent variables. The first independent variable is the presence or absence of using an AOS before viewing videos. The second independent variable included four types of captioning (i.e., on-screen texts) for the videos: full captioning (FC), keyword captioning (KC), glossed keyword captioning (GKC), and glossed full captioning (GFC). The combination of different variables resulted in eight experimental groups: FC + AOS, KC + AOS, GKC + AOS, GFC + AOS, FC, KC, GKC, and GFC. The results reinforced the assertion that an AOS is effective in enhancing incidental vocabulary learning. The assistance provided by the AOS may help L2 learners activate prior knowledge and synthesize important information, which may in turn reduce learners' cognitive processing load for upcoming video information to promote meaningful learning and increased performance when learning different dimensions of vocabulary knowledge. As argued by Mayer (2001), the AOS facilitated L2 learners to outline, organize, and sequence main ideas from watching videos.

Full captioning, compared to keyword captioning, might have provided more information during this study to enable learners to process linguistic and content messages. Primary school L2 learners' enhanced learning of collocations through fully captioned videos seemed plausible, as these students were mostly acquiring L2 vocabulary in a classroom setting and depended on printed materials, compared to native English students for whom learning collocations might be easier due to having more authentic language exposure outside the classroom (Wible, 2008). Full captions possibly helped L2 learners construct links between spoken words and printed words and draw upon background vocabulary knowledge and comprehension strategies to discern potential connections between word form and meaning.

Results showed a significant interaction effect of full captions and advance organizers on incidental learning of collocations. This finding suggests that the L2 young learners obtained substantial collocation knowledge, especially in recognizing form–meaning links. Information presented using the AOS may have helped learners activate their background knowledge and develop a holistic picture of target video materials by discerning upcoming details of the video plot (Li, 2014). In addition, the advance organizer condition may have resulted in more exposure to the collocations. We may need to consider the following implications: focusing on incidental learning of collocations, a more challenging component than single words, is feasible; and young learners, who may have limited cognitive processing compared to L2 adult learners, can be facilitated to learn collocations through captions and advance-organizers.

Reflection

From the investigation in the above-mentioned studies about how learners improved their vocabulary learning from videos, a trend in adopting captioned videos for language learning still seems to be developing. Using captioned viewing in informal settings to allow learners to have choice and control over the videos they watch continues to hold value. I maintain my previous assertion (Teng, 2017) that using videos for flipped classrooms has potential. For example, learners at home can watch videos for tasks that are instructed in the classroom. Likely many challenges in using captioned videos still exist. For example, learners' language proficiency is a determining factor for the effectiveness of captioned videos. Probably one of the critical related issues is the decision to choose captioned videos that will fit with the needs of the students, e.g., their language proficiency. The content of the videos should be slightly above learners' language proficiency level, but still within learners' manageable levels. On the one hand, the videos should challenge learners' abilities, and on the other hand, learners' cognitive load could be reduced because of the facilitation provided by the captions. If the content of the videos is too challenging for comprehension, learners are forced to be dependent on the captions. Screen texts should be appropriate for learners to hone and orchestrate their vocabulary learning strategies. For learners with a low proficiency level, texts should be simple. For learners with intermediate or advanced levels, texts should help learners process phonological, lexico-grammatical, and pragmatic characteristics of the target language. The selection of captioned videos is related to learners' proficiency levels. In my class, learners are motivated to watch an episode from a sitcom, a snippet from a popular movie, or a documentary on a current-events issue. Based on Yeldham (2018), several factors with relation to the selection of captioned videos included whether learners were familiar with the topics; the delivery speed; the linguistic features, including phonological and lexico-syntactic aspects; and whether there was a correspondence between the visual, spoken and captioned cues.

Enlightened by the above studies, teachers can choose some difficult vocabulary/phrases from the captioned videos for the students to practice prior to video viewing. This practice is similar to the advance organizer activity, which is used to bolster learners' comprehension and use of some keywords and sentences in the videos. It may also heighten learners' awareness of new items encountered in the videos. This activity certainly has some disadvantages; for example, reducing the chances that the learners will devise and practice lexical inferencing abilities. However, for learners with a low proficiency level, such activity is helpful. Learners will benefit from teachers' explanations of some keywords, phrases, idioms, and slang that arise in the captioned videos.

In conducting future research examining the effectiveness of captioned videos on vocabulary learning outcomes, long-term experimental studies are necessary. Much of the research carried out so far, including the studies reviewed in this chapter, involved short-term experimental studies. Although the studies considered adding different aspects, e.g., word exposure frequency and advance organizer strategies, to maximize the learning outcomes of using captioned videos, a lot of work still needs to be done. Whether the advantages experienced were from reading the captions, lexical inferencing, listening, or other uncontrolled variables remains unclear. A longitudinal examination of combining quantitative and qualitative analyses is necessary. Within such a design, some standard tests to measure bottom-up skills and vocabulary learning strategies (such as predicting, inferencing, and monitoring abilities), are needed. The various test components would help us draw a fuller picture of learners' vocabulary learning development.

References

Baddeley, A. D. (1986). *Working memory*. New York: Oxford University Press.
Baddeley, A. (2000). The episodic buffer: A new component of working memory? *Trends in Cognitive Sciences*, 4(11), 417–423.
Chung, J. M., & Huang, S. C. (1998). The effect of three aural advance organizers for video viewing in a foreign language classroom. *System*, 26, 553–565.
Fletcher, J. D., & Tobias, S. (2005). The multimedia principle. In R. Mayer (Ed.), *The Cambridge handbook of multimedia learning* (pp. 117–133). Cambridge: Cambridge University Press.
Krashen, S. D. (1985). *The input hypothesis: Issues and implications*. New York: Longman.
Herron, C. A. (1994). An investigation of the effectiveness of using advance organizer to introduce video in the foreign language classroom. *Modern Language Journal*, 78, 190–198.
Hulstijn, J. H. (2001). Intentional and incidental second language vocabulary learning: A reappraisal of elaboration, rehearsal and automaticity. In P. Robinson (Ed.), *Cognition and second language instruction* (pp. 258–286). Cambridge: Cambridge University Press.
Hulstijn, J. H. (2013). Incidental learning in second language acquisition. In C.A. Chapelle (Ed.), *The encyclopedia of applied linguistics* (pp. 2632–2640). Chichester: Wiley-Blackwell.
Li, C. H. (2014). An alternative to language learner dependence on L2 caption-reading input for comprehension of sitcoms in a multimedia learning environment. *Journal of Computer Assisted Learning*, 30, 17–29.
Linebarger, D. L. (2001). Learning to read from television: The effects of using captions and narration. *Journal of Educational Psychology*, 93(2), 288–298.
Markham, P. L., Peter, L. A., & McCarthy, T. J. (2001). The effects of native language vs. target language captions on foreign language students' DVD video comprehension. *Foreign Language Annals*, 34(5), 439–445.
Mayer, R. E. (2001). *Multimedia learning*. Cambridge: Cambridge University Press.
Mayer, R. E. (2009). *Multimedia learning* (2nd ed.). Cambridge: Cambridge University Press.

Montero Perez, M. M., Peters, E., & Desmet, P. (2013). Is less more? Effectiveness and perceived usefulness of keyword and full captioned video for L2 listening comprehension. *ReCALL, 26*, 21–43.

Montero Perez, M., Peters, E., Clarebout, G., & Desmet, P. (2014). Effects of captioning on video comprehension and incidental vocabulary learning. *Language Learning & Technology, 18*, 118–141.

Montero Perez, M. M., Peters, E., & Desmet, P. (2018). Vocabulary learning through viewing video: The effect of two enhancement techniques. *Computer Assisted Language Learning, 31*, 1–26.

National Research Council. (1998). *Preventing reading difficulties in young children*. Washington, DC: The National Academies Press. https://doi.org/10.17226/6023.

Nesselhauf, N. (2005). *Collocations in a learner corpus*. Amsterdam: John Benjamins.

Neuman, S. B., & Koskinen, P. (1992). Captioned television as comprehensible input: Effects of incidental word learning from context for language minority students. *Reading Research Quarterly, 27*, 95–106.

Paivio, A. (1986). *Mental representation: A dual-coding approach*. New York: Oxford University Press.

Pellicer-Sánchez, A. (2017). Learning L2 collocations incidentally from reading. *Language Teaching Research, 21*(3), 381–402.

Peters, E., Heynen, E., & Puimège, E. (2016). Learning vocabulary through audiovisual input: The differential effect of L1 subtitles and captions. *System, 63*, 134–148.

Pulido, D. (2007). The relationship between text comprehension and second language incidental vocabulary acquisition: A matter of topic familiarity? *Language learning, 57*, 155–199.

Rodgers, M. P. H., & Webb, S. (2017). The effects of captions on EFL learners' comprehension of English-language television programs. *CALICO Journal, 34*, 20–38.

Qin, C., & Teng, F. (2017). Assessing the correlation between task-induced involvement load, word learning, and learners' regulatory ability. *Chinese Journal of Applied Linguistics, 40*(3), 261–280.

Schmidt, R. (1990). The role of consciousness in second language learning. *Applied Linguistics, 11*, 129–158.

Schmidt, R. (2001). Attention. In P. Robinson (Ed.), *Cognition and second language instruction* (pp. 3–32). Cambridge: Cambridge University Press.

Schmitt, N. (2010). *Researching vocabulary: A vocabulary research manual*. Basingstoke, England: Palgrave Macmillan.

Siyanova-Chanturia, A., & Spina, S. (2015). Investigation of native speaker and second language learner intuition of collocation frequency. *Language learning, 65*, 533–562.

Taylor, G. (2005). Perceived processing strategies of students watching captioned video. *Foreign Language Annals, 38*(3), 422–427.

Teng, F. (2017). Flipping the classroom and tertiary level EFL students' academic performance and satisfaction. *The Journal of Asia TEFL, 14*(4), 605–620.

Teng, F. (2018a). Incidental vocabulary acquisition from reading-only and reading-while-listening: A multi-dimensional approach. *Innovation in Language Learning and Teaching, 12*(3), 274–288.

Teng, F. (2018b). The effect of focus on form and focus on forms instruction on the acquisition of phrasal verbs by Chinese students. *Asian EFL Journal, 20*(2), 136–164.

Teng, F. (2018c). A learner-based approach of applying online reading to improve learner autonomy and lexical knowledge. *Spanish Journal of Applied Linguistics, 31*, 104–134.

Teng, F. (2019a). Incidental vocabulary learning for primary school students: The effects of L2 caption type and word exposure frequency. *The Australian Educational Researcher, 46*(1), 113–136.

Teng, F. (2019b). *Maximizing the potential of captions for primary school ESL students' comprehension of English-language videos.* Computer Assisted Language Learning, 32(7), 665–691. Doi: 10.1080/09588221. 2018.1532912.

Teng, F. (2019c). *The effects of video caption types and advance organizers on incidental L2 collocation learning.* Computers & Education, 142, 163055. Doi: 10.1016/j.compedu.2019.103655.

Teng, F. (2020). *Vocabulary learning through videos: Captions, advance-organizer strategy, and their combination.* Computer Assisted Language Learning, https://doi.org/10.1080/09588221.2020.1720253.

Teng, F., & Huang, J. (2019). *Predictive effects of writing strategies for self-regulated learning on secondary school learners' EFL writing proficiency.* TESOL Quarterly 53(1), 232–247. https://doi.org/10.1002/tesq.462.

Vanderplank, R. (2016). 'Effects of' and 'effects with' captions: How exactly does watching a TV programme with same-language subtitles make a difference to language learners? *Language Teaching, 49*(2), 235–250.

Webb, S., & Nation, P. (2017). *How vocabulary is learned.* Oxford: Oxford University Press.

Wible, D. (2008). Multiword expressions and the digital turn. In F. Meunier & S. Granger (Eds.), *Phraseology in foreign language learning and teaching* (pp. 163–180). Amsterdam: John Benjamins.

Winke, P., Gass, S. M., & Sydorenko, T. (2010). The effects of captioning videos used for foreign language listening activities. *Language Learning & Technology, 14*, 66–87.

Xu, S., Fang, X. W., Brzezinski, J., & Chan, S. (2008). Development of a dual-modal presentation of texts for small screens. *International Journal of Human-Computer Interaction, 24*(8), 776–793.

Yeldham, M. (2018). Viewing L2 captioned video: What's in it for the listener? *Computer Assisted Language Learning, 31*(4), 367–389.

5   Research Methods for Using Captioned Videos in Incidental Vocabulary Acquisition

This chapter aims to provide recommendations for master and doctoral students about designing, conducting, and reporting high-quality research on incidental vocabulary acquisition from captioned videos. Maximizing incidental vocabulary acquisition from captioned videos is a necessary form of scholarship that can inform theory and practice in L2 vocabulary development. The importance of this research may extend beyond a personal level to include a commitment to enhancing knowledge in this area. EFL teachers may easily become frustrated with the Pied Piper approach, referring to instructional practices promoted with little or no evidence of their effectiveness. High-quality research practices have become essential given teachers' need to understand how to help learners become skilled in learning vocabulary, which is a challenging aspect of L2/EFL acquisition.

This chapter is intended for researchers or research-oriented students seeking a starting point to pursue these practices. I outline five sample research projects from which emerging researchers can develop their skills. Some research designs may be challenging but still achievable. I have sought to provide sufficient background information to clarify the goals and required methodology for each example. Despite being relatively straightforward designs, a more sophisticated mastery of related ideas may be needed to understand the implications of the results fully. The presented research projects do not require a minimum number of participants; in most cases, more is better. Yet if a study is conducted with the intention of developing research expertise based on classroom practice, then a small number of participants may also lead to valuable insight when using the suggested research techniques. However, a sample of roughly 30 participants remains a rule of thumb for classroom practice research when running inferential statistics because a normal distribution of the data must be achieved.

Research Project 1: EFL Students' Perceptions of Using Captioned Videos to Learn Vocabulary

Background

The use of captioning has received a fair amount of attention in EFL teaching and learning contexts. Captions can be used in several ways to promote learning; however, captions may not be provided for all videos and multimedia items. Even when captions are provided, students may not realize that captions are available or maximize vocabulary acquisition through captions. The advantages of using captions include their wide availability and relatively inexpensive access. Learners may use captions in diverse ways to access videos and support their vocabulary learning. However, not all students—especially EFL students—know that captions can be used for vocabulary learning. Investigating learners' understanding of these benefits and limitations would be useful. This research design aims to provide more detailed descriptions of EFL students' attitudinal responses to the use of captions in EFL vocabulary teaching and learning. This type of research is meaningful, as students' attitudes toward the use of captions partially determine what learners will gain from captions. Examining students' responses to captions could thus serve as a basis for more useful language instruction.

Goal

To understand EFL students' responses to having captions as an option for vocabulary learning and the potential benefits and drawbacks of using captions for vocabulary learning.

Research Questions

1 To what extent do various student populations perceive video captions as potentially valuable for their vocabulary learning?
2 How do students use video captions to support their vocabulary learning?

Methodology

A survey containing items scored on a Likert-type scale can be used to analyze EFL learners' perceptions of captioned videos when learning vocabulary. The survey can focus on students' experiences with captions in an online environment. First, exploratory factor analysis through

AMOS or Mplus software can be performed to reduce data to a smaller set of summary variables, explore the underlying theoretical structure of identified phenomena, and identify the structure of relationships between variables. Descriptive analysis, including frequency, means, standard deviations, and medians, should be run on all questions to understand students' responses. The survey should include five to seven variables (e.g., perceived benefits, selection factors, emotional control, and working memory capacity). In addition, items categorized as perceived benefits can focus on classroom use of captions, students' reaction to captions, learners' perceived benefits of using captions for vocabulary acquisition, captions' benefits to comprehension, and students' interest in captioned TV/video material. Items classified as selection factors can focus on learners' perceptions of how to find and use captioned videos to learn vocabulary, learners' attitudes about using captioned videos to learn challenging or unfamiliar words, and learners' attitudes about taking notes on interesting captioned videos to learn more new words. Items classified under emotional control can focus on learners' attitudes when encountering difficult words while viewing captioned videos. Items related to working memory capacity can cover learners' ability for remembering useful words and expressions encountered during captioned viewing and acquiring linguistic knowledge while watching captioned videos. Inferential models (e.g., generalized linear models and multiple regression analyses) can be adapted to analyze the possible influences of numerous variables on learners' vocabulary learning performance after viewing captioned videos.

The second step involves using interviews to explore selected participants' qualitative data and determine how they use captions to acquire vocabulary. Content analysis can be performed to analyze learners' response data. Interview questions can be developed to explore learners' experiences with classroom uses of captioning. Sample questions for exploring learners' perceived disadvantages of captions may include whether learners find captions distracting or as requiring excessive attention; whether learners find it difficult to read, listen to, and watch videos at the same time; the modality of the captions (i.e., closed vs. open captions and pre-recorded vs. live captions); and learners' perceptions of how different modalities affect their vocabulary learning.

Topics for Future Research

1 Similar research design can be applied to explore teachers' perceptions.

2 Qualitative data can include interviews, observations, or both from teachers and students to determine participants' perceptions about what occurred during the captioned video they watched, whether captioning was useful, the strengths and limitations of captioned video viewing, and suggested video modifications.
3 Quantitative research design can be adopted for a large sample of participants to promote the generalizability of the findings.

Research Project 2: Comparing the Effectiveness of Different Vocabulary Teaching Techniques Through Captioned Videos

Background

The emergence of multimedia learning environments offers more opportunities for learners to enhance their vocabulary development. Captioned videos function as a platform to support EFL vocabulary learning. Considerable research has been conducted on adopting captioned videos for vocabulary learning (see a meta-analysis by Montero Perez, Van Den Nootgate, & Desmet, 2013). Based on this meta-analysis and other empirical studies (e.g., Montero Perez, Peters, Clarebout, & Desmet, 2014; Teng, 2019a), two elements are noteworthy when adopting captioned videos for vocabulary learning: (1) the importance of lexical coverage for vocabulary learning and (2) the effectiveness of comprehensible input for such learning. Captions can help learners notice lexical content for vocabulary learning and enhance their understanding of language input, thus helping learners build form–meaning connections in their mental lexicon, which is crucial when learning new words (Van Patten, Williams, & Rott, 2004). Studies have also shown that captions can help learners recognize the meaning of new words (Teng, 2019b; Winke, Gass, & Sydorenko, 2010). These studies serve as valuable references for understanding how captions can be adopted for vocabulary acquisition. However, further research is needed to investigate how captions can be used to stimulate vocabulary learning. While extensive research has addressed the potential of full captioning for acquiring new words, studies have not resolved conflicting results when comparing various caption types (Winke et al., 2010). In line with Guillory's (1998) research, studies have been conducted to compare full captions and keyword captions by reducing textual density (Park, 2004). Disparate results may reflect the importance of attention, a key component of vocabulary learning (Hulstijn, 2001). More studies are needed to explore the effects of salience in the captioning line to stimulate learners' incidental vocabulary learning, which is a by-product of reading or listening activities.

Goal

To compare the effectiveness of different types of captioned videos on learners' acquisition of different types of vocabulary knowledge.

Methodology

The first stage involves reflecting on the participant pool. Using captioned videos for teaching requires students' cooperation, although one can assume that students' interest in video viewing will influence their language learning outcomes. The use of captioned videos is likely best suited to researchers who already teach a class or have access to one. The second stage involves thinking about which types of captions to assess. A common approach consists of comparing the effectiveness of captioning types (e.g., no captioning, fully captioned clips, keyword captioned clips, and fully captioned clips with highlighted keywords; see Montero Perez et al., 2014). Studies exploring the effectiveness of captioning types (e.g., Montero Perez, Peters, & Desmet, 2018; Teng, 2019a, 2019b) have been conducted; however, the rationale for logically comparing captioning types remains ambiguous. For example, it would make sense to compare incidental vocabulary learning performance through different captioning types, learning that accrues from oral versus written captions, or other captioning types used in the researcher's school system. In addition, while examining the effectiveness of captioning on incidental vocabulary learning, more variables can be explored: word exposure frequency, numerous video types, short and long videos, and different word frequency levels in videos.

The next stage involves defining vocabulary learning performance. It is important to consider (a) which word knowledge aspects will be tested (i.e., only the form-meaning link or other aspects, such as derivation knowledge or collocation) and (b) the level of learner mastery required (usually conceptualized as receptive vs. productive mastery). Using an existing test format is likely better than developing a new one, which would be time-consuming and require considerable expertise to do well. The goal is to adapt any instruments to the study (e.g., target lexical items or difficulty level). The next step is to develop a list of target lexical items. The most ecologically sound items would be those that occur in captioned videos but are unknown to participants.

However, controlling for learners' previous knowledge is challenging. The most common approach involves using low-frequency items, although this technique cannot eliminate the possibility that learners may already know the target words. Another technique is using nonwords, but this could lead to validity issues. The third technique entails asking learners to take a pre-test. A limitation of this technique is the possible confounding influence of the pre-test on post-test performance. Researchers may then need to explain how to address this issue in the research design. Methodological comparisons are usually carried out in one of two ways. The first involves using different techniques on the same group of students; in this case, students act as their own controls (i.e., participants display the same attributes across methodologies and possess roughly the same levels of proficiency, aptitude, motivation, and so forth). The second involves using different groups of students, but then the researcher must determine whether students are roughly equivalent in their learning abilities (usually indicated by a proficiency measure or, in the case of lexical acquisition, a vocabulary-size measure). Statistical methods can be adopted to equate groups; ANOVA is a common means of comparing group differences.

Vocabulary gains from different approaches can then be compared. While this comparison can be accomplished by examining descriptive statistics such as means or medians, any differences should be evaluated for normal statistical significance as well. When comparing two techniques, a t-test or nonparametric equivalent may be appropriate. When comparing three or more techniques, then some form of ANOVA or nonparametric equivalent may be required. If participants have different levels of vocabulary proficiency, motivation, working memory, or other variables, researchers may need to use ANCOVA or general linear models to determine the influences of controlled variables on participants' post-test performance. Path analysis can also be used to determine causal models that link independent and dependent variables. Data analysis tends to be challenging but is one of the most rewarding modes of comparison, as it may provide tangible answers regarding which teaching methodologies are most effective for certain types of students.

Topics for Future Research

1   If differences in vocabulary gains are observed, are the differences large enough to be statistically significant for different types of vocabulary knowledge (e.g., form, meaning, and use)? (See Chapter 1 for more details.)

2 If results show slight or significant differences between caption types, does this pattern suggest that student factors (e.g., age, proficiency, motivation, or working memory) may be more important to learning than teaching techniques?

Research Project 3: Exploring the Effects of Captioned Videos on Learning Formulaic Language

Background

Collocation—a type of multi-word unit—has been suggested as a prerequisite for achieving advanced language proficiency and fluency in second-language learning (Schmitt, 2010). Despite efforts to explore best practices in the teaching and learning individual words, research on L2 vocabulary development has only recently begun to examine learning performance with multi-word units, including collocations (Webb & Nation, 2017). L2 learners' acquisition of multi-word units has been found to lag behind single-word acquisition (e.g., Pellicer-Sánchez, 2017); even when learners produce multi-word units, they may demonstrate inappropriate usage (e.g., Nesselhauf, 2005). Moreover, L2 learners may not have sufficient intuition to determine the frequency of collocations and then process or learn them (Siyanova-Chanturia & Spina, 2015). Schmitt (2010) contended that compared to the acquisition of single words, collocations and other multi-word units pose unique challenges for L2 learners. The proposed research design aims to identify collocations in captioned videos and identify effective ways to maximize incidental learning of collocations, namely by adopting an approach to learning vocabulary that focuses learners' attention on discerning the meanings of messages without deliberately committing items to memory (Hulstijn, 2013).

Goal

To understand the larger pattern around collocations and the effects of captioned videos on learning a formulaic language.

Methodology

The first step is to identify and describe formulaic language patterns in captioned videos. A corpus will be needed to query. While extensive corpus resources are available, appropriately captioned videos remain limited. In this research design, using a corpus representing English-language material within various types of captioned videos is likely best. After collecting several sources of captioned videos, the researcher may need to install Concordance and WordSmith to examine the developed corpora. After accessing these resources, a number of target words must be chosen—either a "variety pack" (e.g., words from different word classes with different frequencies and imageabilities) to determine whether lexical patterning varies according to words' characteristics or sets of similar words to determine whether the patterns exhibit any similarities.

The second step is to examine the effectiveness of captioned videos on learning collocations. My innovative study measured the effects of captioned videos on incidental learning of collocations (Teng, 2019a). The study included two independent variables: (1) the presence or absence of an advance-organizer strategy and (2) the type of captioning in videos (i.e., full captioning, keyword captioning, or no captions). Ideas for further replication studies involve two variables: an advance-organizer strategy and captioning type (see Teng, 2020). Research design can include three studies: (1) develop different captioning types and select unknown collocations as target words; (2) design activities based on an advance-organizer strategy and compare results of learning collocations with a control group; or (3) examine the interplay or interaction effects of an advance-organizer strategy and captioning types on learning collocations. In addition, the research design can include different types of videos for L2 learning, such as TV reports, general TV programs, documentary videos, and storytelling videos. Researchers can also assess whether different types of audiovisual input generate distinct effects. Research designs could compare audio input, audiovisual input, and a control group for learning collocations.

Topics for Future Research

1 According to the characteristics of initial target words, are any similarities or differences observed in lexical patterning? (Try to include different types of captioned videos for a larger corpus data source.)
2 Do certain types of collocations present more patterning than others? Do different types of captioned videos produce different results in collocation patterns? (Try to compare TV reports, TV programs, documentary videos, and storytelling videos.)
3 Which approach seems better for helping selected learners learn collocations? What factor(s) might have influenced the results? (Try

to include multiple variables, such as self-regulation, self-efficacy, motivation, vocabulary knowledge, and collocation learning performance, to explore causal relationships between them.)

Research Project 4: Exploring the Repetition of Vocabulary in Captioned Videos

Background

The main factors affecting incidental vocabulary learning performance include target-word frequency (Reynolds & Teng, 2020) and contextual information provided to infer the meaning of target words (Teng, 2019c). Different methods have been used to boost learners' vocabulary through input, such as providing captions to enhance comprehension of audiovisual input (Montero Perez et al., 2018) and increasing encounters with target words (Chen & Teng, 2017). While word features (e.g., recurrences and use of captions) may attract learners' attention and affect the salience of novel words, the use of these features and learners' increased cognizance of the words are only initial steps toward gains in vocabulary knowledge.

Captioned videos may offer a new perspective on exploring incidental vocabulary learning. However, if learners cannot return to a previous word or sentence while watching videos, then vocabulary learning through audiovisual input may be limited due to rapid online processing demands and the difficulties associated with guessing unknown words (Winke et al., 2010). This limitation suggests a need to investigate target-word repetition in captioned videos for incidental vocabulary learning. EFL learners with limited English proficiency tend to avoid printed reading materials and exhibit processing difficulties related to English syntax, vocabulary, phonological representations, inferences, figurative language, and efficient use of short-term memory (Koolstra & Beentjes, 1999). Vocabulary instruction may benefit from an examination of word repetition in captioned videos. Such exploration may reveal theoretical and practical suggestions to enhance EFL students' incidental vocabulary learning.

Goal

To determine whether vocabulary repetition in captioned videos is sufficient to support incidental vocabulary learning.

Methodology

Research suggests that at least ten exposures are required to establish a form-meaning link and develop rich incidental vocabulary knowledge through reading (Webb, 2007). Learning through written input is partially supported by learning through spoken input. In this discussion, "watching captioned videos" refers to receiving simultaneous visual (i.e., reading) and aural (i.e., listening) input. When exploring incidental vocabulary acquisition from reading, graded readers—which are written to maximize vocabulary recycling by limiting the range of vocabulary use and using the principle of repeating vocabulary whenever possible—are often adopted in research design. Some designs have used teenage novels, which follow the principle of repetition to a lesser degree. In all these text types, high-frequency vocabulary is almost always repeated more often than low-frequency vocabulary. This assumption can be extended to the use of captioned videos, particularly storytelling videos for children. This research design is intended to explore vocabulary repetition in several types of captioned videos and to shed light on the implications of repetition (or the lack thereof) for incidental vocabulary learning for L2 learners. The research design can include different types of language input (e.g., audio input, reading input, and audiovisual input from captioned videos as well as including a control group). MANOVA can be performed to explore the effects of several types of language input on vocabulary knowledge performance.

Captioned videos can be provided for L2 learners to read displayed text while watching accompanying videos. The next focus would be to include a variable, such as target-word repetition, to examine the influence of language input effects on vocabulary knowledge acquisition; in this case, a MANCOVA should be performed.

Regarding materials collection for this type of research, texts for L2 young learners should generally be short. Text gathered from the video can be analyzed electronically with a concordance package, the Compleat Lexical Tutor, or the Range program (Heatley, Nation, & Coxhead, 2004). These programs provide frequency lists and identify the amount of repetition and recycling of lexical items within texts. Next, the researcher can choose several target words that have been repeated to varying degrees (i.e., frequently or seldom repeated). For example, how many words would a learner need to read to be exposed to a target word eight times? What types of captioned videos contain enough target words appearing at least eight times? In my experience, many captioned videos may not include target words that appear often enough to allow for close examination. In that case, the text would need to be revised and a native speaker would need to be invited to watch the original video and read the story aloud, matching the predetermined caption speed. The Wondershare Filmora program can be used to replace an original audio track (i.e., stream) with a new audio file created by a native speaker. Alternatively, the researcher can assume a total of 30 target words for the purposes of this project and then calculate how many captioned videos would be needed to reach the 8-exposure threshold for each target word.

Topics for Future Research

1 Do lower-level videos contain more repetition than more advanced ones?
2 What kind of vocabulary is repeated more often in videos? What kind(s) only occurs once or twice?
3 To what extent does target-word repetition influence vocabulary learning performance?
4 How do different captioned video types vary in their overall frequency profiles? How do these profiles affect the suitability of different captioned video types for L2 learners of different proficiency levels?
5 What kind of captioned video would provide sufficient target-word repetition to support incidental vocabulary learning?
6 Which type of language input (reading, listening, or reading-while-listening) requires more exposure for better vocabulary learning performance?

Research Project 5: Vocabulary Learning and Retention Through Multimedia Glossing

Background

Learning vocabulary in a second language is an important basis for language development. Learners benefit from explicit instruction using word lists, vocabulary cards, and glosses. Glosses are marginal short texts that can help learners clarify the meaning of unknown words while reading. In a recent study (Teng, 2019d), glosses were found to facilitate learners' inferences about unknown words and were potentially useful for vocabulary learning. However, the efficacy of different gloss modes remains unknown. Exploring the effectiveness of using simultaneous multimedia learning tools, such as textual, aural, and video animation glossing, on L2 learners' word learning and retention, is particularly necessary (Ramezanali & Faez, 2019). The main focus of this research design is on the effectiveness of multimedia glossing on vocabulary learning and retention. The popularity of multimedia glossing can be attributed to advancements in computer technology and media. In recent years, the integration of glosses into software programs has become an effective way to improve L2 vocabulary performance. In hypermedia environments, multimedia glosses take the form of various vocabulary annotations (e.g., texts, audio, pictures, and video animation). Multimedia glossing presents target words via multiple resource types in a multimedia-based learning setting (e.g., a language lab or classroom equipped with a computer, screen, projector, internet, or other technological tools). Despite acknowledging the effects of multimedia instruction in EFL learning, more research is needed on the use of computer-based glossing, which is an interactive, context-based, and learner-oriented strategy, to facilitate L2 vocabulary acquisition.

Goal

To understand modes of gloss presentation (i.e., L2 definition, aural, and video animation) that are effective for learners' vocabulary learning and delayed word recollection. Research questions can address to what extent glossing modes contribute to L2 learners' immediate and delayed word learning and L2 learners' attitudes toward different glossing modes.

Methodology

The study can be designed as mixed-methods research. The quantitative portion can include experimental groups and one control group. Experimental groups can focus on different glossing modes (e.g., L2 marginal gloss in reading texts, hyperlinked with L2 definition alone; L2 definition and audio glossing; and L2 definition and video animation glossing). The qualitative portion can include data from questionnaires and semi-structured interviews focusing on learners' perceptions of glossing modes. Post-intervention tests can focus on receptive and productive vocabulary knowledge. A pre-test can be administered to examine whether learners already know some target words. Questionnaire items can cover whether glossing modes (a) may help learners learn words and retain meaning and (b) how the learners will use these modes for future learning. Items can be scored on a

5-point Likert-type scale (i.e., 1 = strongly disagree; 2 = disagree; 3 = neither agree nor disagree; 4 = agree; 5 = strongly agree). Interview questions can focus on learners' feelings and experiences when using different glossing modes. The research design can be (5 [five groups] × 2 [two immediate post-tests] × 2 [two delayed post-tests]). A MANOVA can be used for data analysis.

Topics for Future Research

1   One group uses nontraditional hypertexts in which target glossed words are hyperlinked with different multimedia glossing modes. One group uses a traditional reading text with marginal glosses. The assessment can focus on a paper-and-pencil method of assessment as well as a computerized test.
2   Compare dual modes of L2 definition and video animation glossing with single modes of glossing.
3   Measure how learners' working memory capacity affects the five groups' test performance; in this case, a MANCOVA should be used.

Concluding Remarks

Designing a research study is not a straightforward process. It involves a host of interrelated actions: Identifying the purpose, selecting participants, designing treatment and control/comparison conditions, assessments, and statistical methods. Despite the difficulties in designing research, a sound research design is crucial to the understanding of using captioned videos for learning vocabulary. It provides critical information on how to develop, teach, and learn vocabulary through captioned videos. This chapter presents sample research designs to enable researchers to get a glimpse of high-quality intervention research. Each design includes suggestions and guidelines for developing, conducting, and presenting a strong study. Based on Graham and Harris's (2014) recommendations, I created a checklist for doctoral students to reflect on all issues related to designing, conducting, and reporting a high-quality intervention study. The following guidelines serve as a route map for doctoral students to examine the acquisition and retention of vocabulary from captioned videos.

Checklist for Effective Research Design

- The study

- addresses an important theoretical, empirical, and/or practical problem
- includes clearly stated research questions
- includes a hypothesis for each research question
- is designed and carried out in an ethical manner.

- The intervention
  - is theoretically situated
  - draws on previous findings in the research literature on using captioned videos
  - is based on analyses of learners, context, and desired outcomes
  - applies effective instructional methods
  - is piloted (and refined based on the pilot)
  - is described in enough detail to be replicable.

- Instructors/teachers administering the vocabulary learning intervention
  - are provided with lessons for implementing it
  - are provided with guidelines for teaching and learning
  - are taught how to apply it
  - administer it with fidelity during the study.

- The comparison/control condition
  - is credible
  - is similar to the intervention except for features that distinguish it by definition
  - is developed with the same level and care as the writing intervention (see above)
  - is piloted (and refined based on the pilot)
  - is described in enough detail to be replicable
  - is administered with fidelity (data is collected to describe what occurs).

- Each assessment measure
  - is reliable
  - is valid for the purpose to which it is applied
  - does not exhibit floor/ceiling problems
  - is appropriate for the participants' language proficiency level in the study
  - includes equivalent forms (if testing is to occur at more than one time point)

- includes enough samples to provide a valid estimate of performance.
- Statistical analysis
  - fits with the research purpose
  - reliably lends support to the conclusions
  - needs to focus on "differences in nominal significance" occurring in studies with more than one group
  - explains in more detail how to diagnose multicollinearity and use condition indices
  - considers the scale of measurement of the variables to answer the research question.

A thick description of the context is necessary for a qualitative study that aims to generalize the findings. Readers can understand opportunities and constraints in their respective context and determine whether the practice is really effective for their contexts. A thick description of the context can also help learners understand the institutional and sociocultural factors at the micro and macro levels. A qualitative study is to understand teachers' and students' experiences, expectations, values, and motives in using a specific technique. For example, if teachers and students consider a technique for vocabulary learning as time-consuming or too complex, they are unlikely to use such a method even though plenty of studies in support of the technique exist. A quantitative study considers the variables that may influence the findings. The advantage of a quantitative study is the quantification of the data collected. This type of research allows generalizations of the results through a certain sample population. Controlling the variables also requires careful planning of statistical analysis. Indeed, the quantitative study requires extensive statistical analysis. Analyzing quantitative data is difficult for researchers from nonstatistical backgrounds. Statistical analysis is based on scientific discipline and the use of various programs for data analysis. In addition to the traditional program, SPSS, an increasing number of programs, e.g., R, Mplus, and Python, are becoming more influential in the field.

Overall, the purpose of the research design presented in this chapter is to determine whether a technique adopted in the experimental group is effective in enhancing the teaching and learning of vocabulary in a second or foreign language context. There is no guarantee, however, that a vocabulary learning technique that was effective in a series of research studies will be effective in other situations. Achieving a perfect match between the conditions under which a vocabulary learning technique was tested by researchers and the conditions in which it is subsequently applied by those who teach in vocabulary learning courses is not easy. Therefore, more replication studies are needed. The control of more variables can help determine how to transfer evidence-based practices into conventional teaching practices. Otherwise, potentially promising techniques for teaching vocabulary will remain on the shelf to be admired but not used in practice. This chapter presents the sample research designs of high-quality vocabulary learning research. Such a sample research design is a necessary form of scholarship informing theory and practice for future research.

References

Chen, X. N., & Teng, F. (2017). Assessing the effects of word exposure frequency on incidental vocabulary acquisition from reading and listening. *Chinese Journal of Applied Linguistics*, 40(1), 35–52.

Graham, S., & Harris, K. R. (2014). Conducting high quality writing intervention research: Twelve recommendations. *Journal of Writing Research*, 6(2), 89–123.

Guillory, H. G. (1998). The effects of keyword captions to authentic French video on learner comprehension. *CALICO Journal*, 15(1–3), 89–108.

Heatley, A., Nation, I. S. P., & Coxhead, A. (2004). *Range [Computer software] Version 1.32*. Wellington: Victoria University of Wellington. Available from http://www.victoria.ac.nz/lals/staff/paul-nation.aspx.

Hulstijn, J. H. (2001). Intentional and incidental second language vocabulary learning: A reappraisal of elaboration, rehearsal and automaticity. In P. Robinson (Ed.), *Cognition and second language instruction* (pp. 258–286). Cambridge: Cambridge University Press.

Hulstijn, J. H. (2013). Incidental learning in second language acquisition. In C. A. Chapelle (Ed.), *The encyclopedia of applied linguistics* (pp. 2632–2640). Chichester: Wiley-Blackwell.

Koolstra, C. M., & Beentjes, J. W. (1999). Children's vocabulary acquisition in a foreign language through watching subtitled television programs at home. *Educational Technology Research & Development*, 47(1), 51–60.

Montero Perez, M., Peters, E., Clarebout, G. & Desmet, P. (2014). Effects of captioning on video comprehension and incidental vocabulary learning. *Language Learning & Technology*, 18(1), 118–141.

Montero Perez, M., Peters, E., & Desmet, P. (2018). Vocabulary learning through viewing video: The effect of two enhancement techniques. *Computer Assisted Language Learning*, 31(1–2), 1–26.

Montero Perez, M., Van Den Nootgate, W., & Desmet, P. (2013). Captioned video for L2 listening and vocabulary learning: A meta-analysis. *System*, 41(1), 720–739.

Nesselhauf, N. (2005). *Collocations in a learner corpus*. Amsterdam: John Benjamins.

Pellicer-Sánchez, A. (2017). Learning L2 collocations incidentally from reading. *Language Teaching Research, 21*(3), 381–402.

Reynolds, B. L., & Teng, F. (2020). Vocabulary bridge-building: A book review of Norbert Schmitt (2010), I. S. Paul Nation & Stuart Webb (2011), and Paul Meara & Imma Miralpeix (2016). *Applied Linguistics, 41*(4), 612–617, https://doi.org/10.1093/applin/amy021.

Ramezanali, N., & Faez, F. (2019). Vocabulary learning and retention through multimedia glossing. *Language Learning & Technology, 23*(2), 105–124.

Schmitt, N. (2010). *Researching vocabulary: A vocabulary research manual*. Basingstoke, England: Palgrave Macmillan.

Siyanova-Chanturia, A., & Spina, S. (2015). Investigation of native speaker and second language learner intuition of collocation frequency. *Language Learning, 65*(1), 533–562.

Teng, F. (2019a). The effects of video caption types and advance organizers on incidental L2 collocation learning. *Computers & Education, 142*(1), 103655. Doi: 10.1016/j.compedu.2019.103655.

Teng, F. (2019b). Incidental vocabulary learning for primary school students: The effects of L2 caption type and word exposure frequency. *The Australian Educational Researcher, 46*(1), 113–136.

Teng, F. (2019c). The effects of context and word exposure frequency on incidental vocabulary acquisition and retention through reading. *The Language Learning Journal, 47*(2), 145–158.

Teng, F. (2019d). Retention of new words learned incidentally from reading: Word exposure frequency, L1 marginal glosses, and their combination. *Language Teaching Research*. https://journals.sagepub.com/doi/10.1177/1362168819829026.

Teng, F. (2020). Vocabulary learning through videos: Captions, advance-organizer strategy, and their combination. *Computer Assisted Language Learning*, https://doi.org/10.1080/09588221.2020.1720253.

Park, M. (2004). *The effects of partial captions on Korean EFL learners' listening comprehension*. Unpublished doctoral dissertation, Austin, TX: University of Texas at Austin.

Van Patten, B., Williams, J., & Rott, S. (2004). Form-meaning connections in second language acquisition. In B. Van Patten, J. Williams, S. Rott, & M. Overstreet (Eds.), *Form-meaning connections in second language acquisition* (pp. 1–26). Mahwah, NJ: Lawrence Erlbaum.

Webb, S. (2007). The effects of repetition on vocabulary knowledge. *Applied Linguistics, 28*(1), 46–65.

Webb, S., & Nation, P. (2017). *How vocabulary is learned*. Oxford: Oxford University Press.

Winke, P., Gass, S., & Sydorenko, T. (2010). The effects of captioning videos used for foreign language listening activities. *Language Learning & Technology, 14*(1), 65–86.

6 Conclusion

Maximizing Vocabulary Learning Performance From Captioned Videos

Captioning refers to the process of converting audio content into text and displaying the text of a video on a screen. Alongside the emergence of technology, the environment of learning English as a foreign language has moved into a new era of using authentic audiovisual materials. In recent years, access to technology such as television, DVDs, video equipment, and computers has expanded. Captions are increasingly used in foreign language classes given growing accessibility to video media platforms such as YouTube. Captioning renders audio and audiovisual material accessible and provides learners critical links to communication, information, education, news, and entertainment. Captions can also enhance learners' comprehension and fluency when using English. In addition, captions can help improve the literacy skills of children and adults alike. A growing number of classroom practitioners have begun to consider audiovisual teaching materials appropriate for students at all levels of foreign language learning. Various TV programs have become a daily part of students' studies and lives. However, many teachers worry that learners benefit little from these ungraded materials, particularly when learners do not have enough linguistic knowledge to process the input. In an attempt to overcome this gap, captions may be used to help learners conduct dual processing of audio and visual input. Captions can thus serve as a useful means of improving learners' aural comprehension.

In this book, I have sought to cover major themes that I consider essential to vocabulary learning from captioned viewing in a second or foreign language learning. The primary purpose is to provide readers a better understanding of the nature of captions for EFL teaching and learning. I hope I have explained the issues associated with using captions for learning vocabulary well. Captions can be of real educational and linguistic benefit to language learners. Although this book only provides a brief description of captions and their applications, I am confident the benefits presented in this book provide compelling evidence for adopting captioned viewing as an essential part of the equality and accessibility agenda for L2 and EFL learners in many parts of the world. Captioned video viewing differs from watching TV programs and films. In this book, by summarizing the key motives behind using captioned viewing for vocabulary learning, I seek to reinforce the claim that captioned videos can occupy their own space in the current L2 and EFL learning environment.

Perceptions of Using Captioned Videos in EFL Context

Although this book presents key research findings in studies using captioned videos for vocabulary learning, relative ignorance toward using captions remains. Some teachers may still suggest that viewing standard TV programs is sufficient for language learning. As an EFL learner myself, I fully understand the frustration of attempting to get the gist of a foreign-language TV program without captions. In addition, vocabulary learning requires a deep form–meaning link (Schmitt, 2010; Teng, 2019a); hence why vocabulary acquisition is one of the most challenging parts of language learning. Therefore, TV programs without captions are not sufficient for learning vocabulary in an EFL context. Captioned films and programs, for example, should be used to raise learners' language awareness when processing target vocabulary words.

This book is a response to the growth of captioning in various forms and formats. More captioned TV programs are available than ever before. Captioned viewing has also become popular because of advances in technology. However, using captioned viewing for language learning, including vocabulary acquisition, remains overlooked. I recently visited primary schools in Hong Kong, most of which adopted printed materials for English learning. Captioned videos were solely intended for leisure, not learning. Also, captioned TV programs were not widely available at these schools, and teachers did not provide captioning on educational videos. Captioned educational videos are more prevalent in schools with students who are deaf or hard of hearing. At a talk regarding the possible use of captioning in videos, many teachers stated that watching videos was not useful for language teaching in the classroom; using too many videos did not fit with their teaching guidelines or work schemes stipulated by the education bureau. In addition, teachers were at a loss as to how to create captions, a process that seemed laborious and skill intensive. Teachers believed that using videos for teaching would cause students to ignore essential

Conclusion

parts of the course. The same could be said for students: many learners may lack the motivation to watch captioned videos outside of class. As reported by Vanderplank (2016), many learners considered captioned video viewing as a leisure-oriented pastime rather than a serious learning exercise. Some learners were resistant to such out-of-class assignments. Much work thus remains to be done before teachers and students can recognize and agree upon the potential of using captioned videos for language learning.

Creating Captions for Videos

Numerous methods are available for creating captions for videos. A common one is Amara (https://amara.org/zh/videos/create/), a community-based subtitle and translation website. Users can submit videos for free subtitling or captioning. The first step is to upload a video to YouTube, Vimeo, or Canvas. Users can also link videos already published to Vimeo or YouTube. The second step is to send the video to Amara. For videos on YouTube or Vimeo, users must copy the full video URL to the clipboard, go to Amara, click "Subtitle video" at the top, and paste the URL. Once the video is uploaded, it can be edited by clicking on the "Improve subtitle" button and then using the subtitle editor (Figure 6.1).

When inserting captions into videos, specific details should be kept in mind. Captions (1) should be synchronized and appear at approximately the same time as the audio is delivered; (2) should be equivalent in content to that of the audio, including speaker identification and sound effects; and (3) should be of sufficient size and contrast to ensure readability in addition to being timely, accurate,

Figure 6.1 Captioning Through Amara.

98 Conclusion

complete, and efficient. Although captioning may seem daunting at first, after trying it once, the process is relatively simple and efficient. Also, providing alternatives to audio options when using video media is highly advised to meet the needs of students with hearing-related disabilities. Still, it can benefit all students, particularly those learning a foreign language. After becoming familiar with useful options, such as using YouTube's automatic captions or Amara's free services, captioning should become easier. Captioning only needs to be done once, and the benefits make it well worth the effort. Other free ways to caption videos are available, such as YouTube's new version of Creator Studio called YouTube Studio: find a video to caption or subtitle, select the "Edit" drop-down menu beside the video, and select "Subtitles/CC." Understanding how to add captions to videos is essential for teachers.

Challenges in Using Captioned Videos

Challenges will inevitably arise when using captioned videos. A central problem is that learners' language proficiency can influence their learning when watching captioned videos. Several studies have included low-proficiency learners as participants (e.g., Pujolà, 2002; Sydorenko, 2010). Pujolà (2002) worked with a multi-proficiency cohort of less-proficient, intermediate, and upper-intermediate learners. Data from multiple sources (i.e., observations, verbal reports, and interviews) indicated that less-proficient learners focused on reading the captions, considering them a crutch for understanding aural input. However, in another study involving a multi-proficiency cohort (Taylor, 2005), many lower-proficiency learners were overloaded when simultaneously attending to the visual, caption, and speaker cues. Determining how to overcome these problems was also difficult. By contrast, the more proficient learners in Pujolà's (2002) study tended to rely on captions to help them overcome comprehension difficulties. In addition, the more proficient learners in Taylor's (2005) study reported their capabilities in attending to verbal, caption-based, and other visual cues mostly simultaneously. Teng (2019b) also found learners' language proficiency to play a vital role in the way learners engage with captioned videos.

Presumably, low-proficiency learners can be expected to pay attention to captions by reading them, while higher proficient learners should be able to engage more fully with multiple cues provided by speakers in videos. Mayer's (2009) cognitive load theory posits that learners can process a finite amount of information in a channel simultaneously, and they must discern incoming information by creating mental representations. The cognitive load theory highlights five key features. First, a learners' mind can process information better when it is not overloaded. For example, higher-proficiency students generally process information better than low-proficiency students. Adopting Vandergrift's (2003) metacognitive model, high-proficiency learners strategically coordinate cognitive resources to compensate for comprehension difficulties. They can also adapt available resources to plan, monitor, and evaluate their comprehension. As Teng and Huang (2019) reported, learners with higher proficiency are more likely to adopt metacognitive strategies for better performance. Although Teng and Huang's (2019) study was situated in an EFL writing context, findings may provide insight into the use of captioned videos for vocabulary learning, as learning vocabulary and learning to write naturally connected. Second, learners with low proficiency may find captioned videos challenging, and they may find it challenging to comprehend video content given their cognitive limitations. Due to the short time for which text appears on the screen, learners with low proficiency may favor reading captions over attending to spoken cues. Third, constraints on a learner's working memory in processing information may apply. Working memory helps learners guide their learning-related decision making and behavior. Students with low proficiency may have a lower level of working memory; this lack of working memory capacity may influence their performance when learning vocabulary from captioned videos. Fourth, learners may process aural and visual information through separate channels (Paivio, 2007). Low-proficiency learners can overload their visual conduit when processing video images and captioned texts simultaneously. Finally, learning performance may differ based on the genre of captioned videos. For instance, sports, animation, and nature programs may pose various difficulties for learners. For example, in Taylor's (2005) study, low-proficiency students reported the nature/documentary genre of captioned videos as being particularly challenging. Videos with captioned texts that remain on screen for longer and are easier to decipher would be better suited for information and meaning processing.

I do not mean to contend that captioned videos would be inappropriate for low-proficiency students; instead, I recommend adopting captioned videos for these students. But it is essential to consider how to choose captioned videos, particularly those that are appropriate for students' proficiency. In selecting appropriate videos to enhance learners' vocabulary acquisition in a foreign language context, some conditions need to be met. First, teachers should choose videos that challenge learners' abilities, although captions should also help learners reduce their cognitive load to a manageable level. Second, captions should not exceed learners' proficiency to the extent that learners must rely solely on captions to comprehend the input. Learners should instead be able to hone their linguistic skills and strategies. Third, teachers should use simplified texts as captions for videos to suit their students' levels. In designing texts, teachers may need to take authentic phonological, lexico-grammatical, and pragmatic characteristics into account. Finally, teachers should select videos to refine learners' abilities by orchestrating various strategies to develop comprehension. When captioning helps learners reflect on their linguistic strategy use, they may become better skilled at simultaneously processing different cues to build deeper form–meaning mapping of new words or structures in the text.

Future Practice in Using Captioned Videos

In the future, understanding learners' capabilities in using captioned videos and their prior experiences with captions would be helpful. We must also bear in mind that learners who have used captioned videos for a long time may become overly reliant on them. Learners who develop entrenched viewing habits may struggle to transfer these abilities to settings where captions are unavailable. We may therefore need to consider the possibility of integrating learners' exposure to captioned texts with regular exposure to uncaptioned listening. Another approach is to use advance-organizer strategies (i.e., previewing activities and teachers' explanations for some difficult vocabulary/phrases), as was adopted in recent studies (Teng, 2019c, 2020). Based on my work, the advance-organizer strategy was helpful in scaffolding learners' comprehension and raising their awareness of target items in the text. Some may criticize this strategy, claiming it could hinder learners' chances to practice inferring target words' meanings from context. I agree with Yeldham's (2018) assertion that eye tracking is a necessary technique in understanding learners' gaze while viewing videos. When learners watch captions, they may not necessarily be reading them. We may need to understand better how captions do or do not attract learners' gazes. Current eye-tracking devices allow for head and body movements to be monitored along with the viewer's eye fixations. Yeldham (2018) pointed out that much of the research thus far has involved short-term experimental studies with a focus on the outcomes of captioned versus non-captioned viewing. Results have mostly supported the use of captioned viewing. However, it remains unclear whether this advantage was based on reading captions or listening to the speakers. We may need eye-tracking devices to examine learners' viewing behavior. Insights from eye-tracking experiments can also be supplemented by semi-structured interviews or stimulated recalls to extract additional information.

Over the years, I have heard many encouraging stories about using captioned videos for language learning. In one account, a friend of mine told me his daughter had spent a good deal of time picking up words and phrases from TV programs. Based on our discussion, watching captioned videos or programs was key to his daughter's language development. In another account, an EFL adult learner told me she used captioned comedies, operas, and nature programs to learn key words and began to communicate with native speakers in English. My six-year-old daughter has also greatly benefited from watching captioned TV programs. Chinese was her first language, but later I found out that she used more English than Chinese. When she had difficulty figuring out a Chinese word, she would use English words to express the Chinese meaning. To maximize the potential of captioned viewing, I adopted previewing and reviewing activities to help her learn vocabulary words prior to or after viewing. Such strategies may also help maximize her language learning performance.

Undoubtedly, readers of this book may have had similar language learning experiences. If captioned viewing has not yet been considered in a certain reading context, I would encourage readers to try them to potentially discover the transformative potential of this add-on technique originally intended for the deaf and hard of hearing. The primary challenge is to seize the potential of using captioned videos for language learning. Additional research along this line of study is necessary. We also need more support for using captioned viewing for language teaching and learning around the world.

References

Mayer, J. (2009). *Multimedia learning* (Second Ed.). Cambridge: Cambridge University Press.

Paivio, A. (2007). *Mind and its evolution: A dual coding theoretical approach*. Mahwah, NJ: Erlbaum.

Pujolà, J.-T. (2002). CALLing for help: Researching language learning strategies using help facilities in a web-based multimedia program. *ReCALL*, 14, 235–262.

Schmitt, N. (2010). *Researching vocabulary: A vocabulary research manual*. Basingstoke: Palgrave Macmilla.

Sydorenko, T. (2010). Modality of input and vocabulary acquisition. *Language Learning and Technology, 14,* 50–73.

Teng, F. (2019a). Retention of new words learned incidentally from reading: Word exposure frequency, L1 marginal glosses, and their combination. *Language Teaching Research.* https://journals.sagepub.com/doi/10.1177/1362168819829026.

Teng, F. (2019b). *Maximizing the potential of captions for primary school ESL students' comprehension of English-language videos.* Computer Assisted Language Learning, 32(7), 665–691. Doi: 10.1080/09588221.2018.1532912.

Teng, F. (2019c). *The effects of video caption types and advance organizers on incidental L2 collocation learning.* Computers & Education 142(1), 103655. Doi: 10.1016/j.compedu.2019.103655.

Teng, F. (2020). *Vocabulary learning through videos: Captions, advance-organizer strategy, and their combination.* Computer Assisted Language Learning. https://doi.org/10.1080/09588221.2020.1720253.

Teng, F., & Huang, J. (2019). Predictive effects of writing strategies for self-regulated learning on secondary school learners' EFL writing proficiency. *TESOL Quarterly, 53,* 232–247.

Taylor, G. (2005). Perceived processing strategies of students watching captioned video. *Foreign Language Annals, 38,* 422–427.

Vandergrift, L. (2003). Orchestrating strategy use: Toward a model of the skilled second language listener. *Language learning, 53*(3), 463–496.

Vanderplank, R. (2016). *Captioned media in foreign language learning and teaching.* London: Palgrave Macmillan.

Yeldham, M. (2018). Viewing L2 captioned videos: What's in it for the listening? *Computer Assisted Language Learning, 31*(4), 367–389.

Index

active processing assumption 21
advanced organizer strategies 56, 85, 100
affective filter 20
associations 6
attrition 8–9
audiovisual input 12, 86

bimodal input 12, 15

captioned videos 5, 11, 15, 16, 17, 18, 20, 38, 53, 54, 55, 73, 74, 79, 80, 86, 95, 96, 100
captioning 95, 96, 98
captions 15, 18, 19, 36, 41, 53, 79, 86, 95
central executive 22–3
chunking ability 21
Cognitive Load Theory 25–6, 98, 99
collocation 2–3, 67, 84
comprehensible input 81
consciousness 20
contentcomprehension 40, 42

depth of vocabulary knowledge 6
dual-channel assumption 21
dual-coding theory 24–5
dual-modal presentation technique 28, 29

engagement 9–10, 48
English as a foreign language (EFL) 1, 79

evaluation 9–10
extraneous cognitive load 17, 21
eye tracking 100
flipped classrooms 73
fluency 1
form 2–3
form-meaning link 6, 7, 8, 10, 54, 87, 96
form–meaningmapping 100
frequency 6, 80

glosses 88, 89
grading factors 26–30
grammar functions 2
grammatical patterns 6

high-frequency vocabulary 87

incidental vocabulary acquisition 5, 6, 7, 8, 11, 16, 78
individual differences 2–3
Input Hypothesis 20–1
intentional vocabulary learning 5

language awareness 96
lexical development 9–10
lexical inferencing 79
lexical items 4
lexical knowledge 7–8
limited capacity assumption 21
long-termmemory 21
low-frequency vocabulary 87

marginal glosses 5
meaning 2–3
metacognitive model 99
metacognitive strategies 99
motivation 51
multimedia learning environment 81
multimedia learning theory 21–2
multimedia principle 21
multi-word units 82

need 9–10

phonological loop 22–3
productive knowledge 2–3
proficiency level 9, 66, 74
pronunciation 2

receptive knowledge 2–3
register 6
retention 8, 11, 48

sensory memory 21

search 9–10
selection factors 26–30
self-regulated vocabulary learning 10
short-term memory 86
spelling 2
split-attention effect 25
spoken form 6

task 3

use 2–3

visual cues 98
visuospatial sketchpad 22–3
vocabulary knowledge 1, 6, 9, 56
vocabulary learning strategies 10, 74

word exposure frequency 56, 82
working memory 9, 21, 22, 23, 25, 80, 99
written form 6